THAT DOLL GINNY

By

Jeanne Du Chateau Niswonger, AB., MA., PhD.

Photographs by the author, Vogue Dolls, Inc., and others as credited

1983 Revised Edition

Printed by: Cody Publications, Kissimmee, FLorida

Address all inquiries to:

Jeanne Niswonger
305 West Beacon Road
Lakeland, Florida 33803

DEDICATION

TO: VIRGINIA GRAVES CARLSON, the first Ginny and my collaborater, for without her memories of Ginny as designer for Vogue for over 20 years, this book could not have been written. I am deeply indebted to her for the use of many old Vogue photographs, records, price lists, catalogs and booklets as well as information and photographs from her own family albums. In this manner, too, she is author of the book.

ACKNOWLEDGMENTS

TO: MARGE MEISINGER, whose interest in Ginny as a collector gave impetus to the creation of this book. I am especially grateful to her for sending me boxes of dolls over a period of many years so that I could study and photograph them.

TO: LIA SARGENT: who gave me encouragment to write the book and assisted in many ways through correspondence, research, pictures and information.

TO: MARGE MAGINNIS, who did the art work on the patterns and clothing labels.

TO: EDWIN W. NELSON, JR., President of Vogue Dolls, Inc., from 1961 to 1976, for his assistance in providing information and photographs and keeping me informed on the production of Ginny dolls.

TO: VOGUE DOLLS, Inc., a subsidiary of Lesney Products Corporation, for use of current promotional material on the Ginny doll.

TO: GENEVIEVE Du CHATEAU CRAWFORD, my sister, who provided invaluable assistance in layout work and proofreading the manuscript.

TO: JO ANN ZIPPERER, for sharing her dolls with me and providing information.

TO: Members of the Ginny Doll Club and others who have helped over the years. It would be impossible to list all names and I hope that I have not commited the sin of omission as so many have provided information and help but here are some who have been especially helpful in several ways:

Ann Bergin   Sonny Hemmi
Marie Blair   Rose McDonald
Jeannette Cain   Loette McLinn
Bessie Carson   Eunice Peterson
Phyllis Clark   Aurelia Rupert
Judy Curtis   Pat and Dwight Smith
Jennie Davis   Ferdinande Steadman
Elizabeth Donoghue, Curator of Dolls,   Eloise Thomas, Director,
                    Wenham Museum   Yesteryear Museum

CONTENTS

Hi! I'm Ginny

Vogue photo

INTRODUCTION

This book has been on my mind for a long time. It is primarily a long term research project compiled over a number of years of study and searching for information. It has not been easy as early records are lacking. Vogue Dolls was, of course, in the business of producing dolls as toys and no one thought much about keeping records through the years with research in mind. The plant moved several times over the years, and quite naturally, many things were discarded in the process. I was fortunate in making contact with Virginia Carlson, Vogue's designer, who had managed to salvage some of the old photographs and records of the company, and I am very appreciative of having the use of this material. This, together with bits and pieces here and there has enabled me to reconstruct an outline of the history of Vogue Dolls and Ginny.

Often I am asked how many different costumes were made for Ginny. I have accounted for several hundred and am still searching for others. Some outfits never appeared in any catalog or booklet, perhaps hundreds even, as Vogue made up special garments for several of the big mail order houses for decades. At any rate, I would say that there are well over one thousand items of clothing made for Ginny since her beginning.

I know that a number of readers will be disappointed that I have not included a price guide but I feel that the inclusion of pricing quickly outdates a book. As stated above, my efforts have been directed toward creating a resource book on Vogue and Ginny that would be of value to the interested doll collector or dealer. Pricing information is generally available in other books. Actually, the price would vary a great deal depending upon how rare the doll is or her costume, plus the condition such as 'played with' or mint in a box. In the final analysis, the price you pay is what the doll is worth to you and how much you are willing to invest in it. As for resale, the actual price you paid should be your guide along with how much profit you need to make. There is information on the original prices in this book that can serve as a guide in determining how much a particular item is worth and remembering to take into consideration today's inflationary prices.

I had hoped to reprint more of the young girls' GINNY DOLL NEWS of the 1950's but space did not permit. They are indeed a fine memento of Ginny. The little paper did contain quite a bit of non doll material such as puzzles, contests, names of contest winners, seasonal and historical stories, etc., that was not pertinent to Ginny or related to dolls. However, I have utilized some of the information contained in them.

Alliteration was used in the naming of Ginny and her immediate family members; Jill, Jan, Jimmy, Jeff and Ginnette. They were created by a fine lady named Jennie and her daughter was named Ginny who had a sister named June. People have pointed out to me that I just seem to belong, too, with my name Jeanne (pronounced Jean or in French, Jahn). Not many folks know that I have a sister named Jenny who has sons, Joe and George. I married a Joe and my son married Virginia whom he calls his 'real, live Ginny doll' and their new baby was named Jeanne. And, while I was researching this book, a tiny baby orphan otter came to live with me and she was promptly named GINNY!

It is my hope that readers will enjoy this book and that it will be of value as a source of reference. I have tried to give accurate information while at the same time relating a little of the personal side of my long fascination with Ginny. She is a very special doll and the people who have produced her are very special people.

Baby otter named GINNY

IN THE BEGINNING

Ever since I can remember I have always
loved dolls, miniatures, stuffed animals and real live little creatures, too.
The holiday season just wouldn't have
been Christmas unless there was a new
doll under the tree, and Santa always
remembered to bring the doll that I
wanted from having peeked at them be-
forehand in the toy department in the
downtown stores. My sister and I played
with dolls until we were quite old; into
the teen years, I'm sure. So, between
us we had a nice collection of dolls.
Often our birthdays brought a new small
doll and stuffed animals were part of
our Easter Basket. We were fortunate
that our parents realized the play
value that dolls afforded children and
they took an active part in our play life
by helping, such as our mother making
new clothes for the dolls and our
father constructing doll houses and
furniture for us. They often brought
us some little doll trinket or miniature, too, on Saturday shopping trips
and we always looked forward to their
return to see what they had brought
us. We always had household pets, too,
in our growing up years; little kittens,
puppies, bantam chickens and bunnies
and they provided valuable learning
experiences. So, it was only natural
that when I reached adulthood I had,
among other things, two very consum-
ing interests: Dolls and wildlife
conservation. At first, the two do

The author, age two, and Teddy Bear

not seem especially compatible, but they are united by one word: PRESERVATION.
As some people like to see old houses or antique items preserved, my interests
centered around the preservation of old and collectible dolls as a symbol of our
cultural and historic heritage. And, my lifelong interest in animals led me to
become active in the ecology movement long before it became a household word.
I've worked for preservation of wilderness and wildlife since the 1950's, and am
still active in this field today.

Although most of my childhood dolls were given away, I managed to keep a few of
them, and still have them in my collection today. For a while, I did nothing
about collecting dolls; somewhere in my teens, I put them aside as most girls do,
for other maturing interests. But even so, periodically I found myself buying
one now and then and tucking it away, even though I didn't recognize that I was
a collector, or rather I should say, admit that I was. I had a few old ones
that belonged in the family and every once in a while I found myself buying one
that reflected my interest in foreign lands and other cultures. I remember
going across the border to Mexico and coming back with a small doll dressed in
a serape and sombrero; still another one was a Carmen Miranda doll in gaily
decorated outfit, and I was pleased to find one made by native Eskimos from
Alaska.

5

MY FIRST VOGUE DOLL

During World War II, I visited New York City which was a thrilling experience for a young girl. Amidst all the attractions and things to do in such a great metropolis, I found myself wandering to the toy sections of the wonderfully large department stores, and looking at the counters lined with dolls. I told myself that I was through playing with dolls and that I didn't need them anymore. But, I still felt an irrestible attraction to them.

One day, while reading the newspaper I noticed a large advertisement for a new shipment of dolls that had just come in. It is interesting to report that I had more or less ignored the screaming headlines about the War and was concentrating on the lovely pictures of the dolls in the ad. I just had to go to that toy department and look at the dolls myself. At the store there was quite a large display of Vogue dolls in all kinds of little costumes from Far-Away Places, Fairy Tales and little childrens' clothes. I looked at them for a long time and although I would have liked to buy several, my allowance was limited and I

Indian boy, Vogue's composition Ginny or Toddles

knew that I must decide on just one. I finally selected an eight inch one attired in an American Indian outfit with long black braids, a necklace of wooden beads and complete with Indian headdress and feathers. His right arm was bent at the elbow and his arms, legs and heads all have moving parts. He had blue eyes, glancing to the right; an Indian with blue eyes? Well, no matter, he surely was cute. VOGUE was marked on his back and at the time there was a little round paper sticker attached to his garment which read VOGUE also. The name Vogue had no special meaning to me at the time. Much later I was to learn that this was a compostion Ginny or Toddles. That war time year of 1943 marks the exact time that I first acquired a Vogue doll. Little did I realize that it was only a small beginning of things to come. And, looking back, I've always wondered if my selecting the American Indian was not symbolic in some way; the first true American. Perhaps he reflected my faith in our country during the terrible war that was eventually to come to a victorious end.

Anyway, the little Indian doll moved around with me everywhere I went for a great number of years. Sometimes he just stayed in a box or was tucked away in a drawer. In a way he represented my dormant interest in dolls that I almost completely repressed as a young adult. It wasn't until after I was married and had three children including two daughters that I rediscovered the little Indian fellow. And so, he came out of hiding in the late 1950's when my girls were playing with dolls. And this is the beginning of my long love affair with Ginny.

A NOSTALGIC CHILDHOOD

The first dolls that my two little girls received were GINNY DOLLS that were given to them by their grandfather when they were babies. (The same father who had made doll houses and furniture for me.) They spent many happy days playing with Ginny in a houseful of real wooden furniture and accessories including a great variety of clothing items for them. And best of all, my daughters had a whole family of dolls to play with for the Ginny family members included little sister and brother, Ginnette and Jimmy as well as Jill, Jeff and Jan. How I would have loved these when I was small as I had always longed for a boy doll. My girls had a special room upstairs that was converted into a walk-in Ginny doll house and all the little girls in the neighborhood came to play in it.

When my daughters were very small their play with dolls just consisted of dressing and undressing them, putting them to bed and, of course, the ritual of feeding them, just as all little girls do. Then with the addition of Ginny's little brother and sister as well as dolls that represented mother and father figures, my girls' play horizons broadened. They learned to be neat through hanging up the dolls' clothes, putting shoes in the closet, making beds and picking up their toys. There were little lessons in getting along with other people and the usual give and take necessary among family members. The doll play very much paralleled events in their own everyday life. Later as they approached the teen years, they began to sew for the doll family and a whole new world of fashion, materials and construction was opened up to them.

Indeed the Ginny dolls served them well through the years and often accompanied them to school to represent some special lessons in social science, geography, literature or history, for their outfits included patriotic, historical, storybook and international. There were valuable lessons learned, too, about our own American culture and background for Ginny was made in the image of a real little girl. Although some collectors only like to see Ginny dressed as a small child, all her little costumes are appropriate if you just stop and think about it. What little girl does not relish dressing up in mommy's fine clothes and high heeled shoes and play grown up? And, think of the children who jump at a chance to enact a make believe role in a school play. And look how every small child loves to play cowboy and Indians in appropriate outfits or take on a new identity at Halloween. There never was a little girl who didn't love to dress up as a bride or raid grandmother's trunk in the attic. And, part of the fun in taking dancing lessons is the various costumes that the little dancer gets to don in the course of recitals and shows.

Psychiatrists and child psychologists have made interesting observations on why dolls have such a phenomenal place in the hearts of girls, almost since time immemorial. For one thing dolls, such as Ginny, strike a common denominator as the all-American good little girl that the child can identify with and also want to be like her. As their personalities grow, chidren almost since time began, have used things to develop their fantasies around and girls in particular have chosen objects which they love and kiss, mainly dolls. Part of this is imitative behavior for they do to dolls what they see their mothers doing to them or siblings. Girls also imagine that they are grown up as they practice the adult role of woman and mother. Ginny represented a contemporary individual and can be almost anything to the child such as a baby, a little girl or a teen-ager according to the girl's desires. Ginny enabled millions of little girls to put themselves into almost a limitless future life situation and through her they were able to project myriad young adult or teen age lives according to the costume the child chose to dress Ginny in for the time. Thus, Ginny also represented the girl's hopes and dreams for the future.

It is interesting to reflect here on our own childhood play with dolls. We don't even realize it at the time, but later in life do gain insight into how very important doll play is in every girl's life. She is born with an instinct to mother and her play role of mothering dolls prepares her well for later when she is a real mother. Still other things are learned from doll play that help us prepare for life's long venture. There are dolls to represent every creed and color and we gain a tolerance of other races and cultures and an understanding of the whole history of mankind. We, as adult collectors, especially learn an appreciation of the doll as an art form through making a new doll or construction of its clothing. The costume alone can be appreciated because of the beauty of the fabric or unique style which again records man's adornment of himself down through the ages. Let's not overlook dolls as a satisfying craft with its aspect of molding, creating a new face, clothing construction, repairing, wig making and the use of miniatures that usually is associated with dolls. Through the study and research of dolls, one can be involved in experiences in many fields such as religion, the theater, manners, modern and primitive art, child psychology, anthropology, economic conditions of the world, textiles and crafts, sociology, evolution of the human race and the development of human culture.

And so my interest in dolls was unleashed during my daughter's childhood doll play. I relished the role of doll buyer for them and in helping them find new little outfits and in setting up the Ginny doll house. Then, there came a time, too, when their maturing years took on new interests. I started to pack away the Ginny dolls for possible use of grandchildren. I remember wondering whether or not to even keep them. It wasn't long after this that I was chairman of a civic group's dinner meetings which had an international theme. Looking for ideas to use for decorations and centerpieces, I remembered the Ginny dolls packed away in all their cute little frocks. They were a perfect size for table decorations. From then on the Ginnys were mine and I began to add to the collection, becoming more interested in learning about the history of the dolls and this was finally launched into a long term research project.

It was at this point that I heard of doll clubs and then joined the United Federation of Doll Clubs, Inc.,a national organization with over 10,000 members today and almost 500 clubs. No wonder there are so many collectors; it is number two collecting hobby in this country now with only stamp collectors outnumbering the doll collecting hobby. I remember giving a program on Ginny for the Tampa Doll Club in 1972 after I had begun the long-term research project on Vogue dolls. About this time, I had also joined some of the corresponding doll clubs, that is those with a newsletter, and I'd acquired a number of pen pals who were interested in Ginny and closely related dolls. We were writing back and forth so much that it seemed like a good idea to start a corresponding club pertaining to Ginny and Vogue dolls. So, the year 1973 saw the Ginny Doll Club come into existence and it has been thriving ever since.

MY GINNY DOLLS

When I see my Ginny dolls lined up in a row,
I hear a voice call "Mama' from the long, long ago;
A little girl I knew so well who trotted after me.

"I really need some lace" she'd say,"for Ginny, don't you see?"
A pretty lady she is now with children of her own,
And I sew lace on Ginny's clothes since Ginny's Mom is grown.

Marion Line

GINNY, THE LIBERATING DOLL

Lia Sargent is a New Yorker who is a discriminating collector of Ginnys and Vogue family dolls. A former teacher, she holds a master's degree in education and once worked with exceptional children. Now married to a professor of English literature, her husband, Robert, takes quite an interest in her collecting. It was Lia who first suggested that Ginny was the liberating doll and that she was a symbol of unisex before the word was invented. Certainly all of her little outfits were positive proof of this for she was equally at home in blue jeans, overalls or cowboy boots as she was in the frilliest formals, dancing frocks or debutante gowns.

Lia also pointed out that Vogue never found it necessary to introduce a separate boy doll to go with Ginny but used the same doll to represent little males, dressing him as cowboys, Dutch or Swiss boys. Vogue provided Ginny with a whole range of outfits so that her little owners through her could fantasize themselves in many activities and diversified role playing. A doll before her time, Ginny was a real pacesetter and many doll companies copied Vogue's original ideas of an active little doll ready for anything such as camping, skating, swimming or playing tennis. She could also make a quick change of identities and the little girl who played with her would delight in dressing her up as a ballerina, nun or nurse or put her in a foreign costume or outfit from Fairyland. "There were no limitations imposed because of her sex", said Lia about Ginny. "In today's world with the feminist movement gaining momentum some women feel that dolls are irrelevant to any important issue concerning women, while others even condemn dolls as sexist and role restricting. So many women would be surprised to learn that Ginny was an important facet behind today's woman's movement and their own independence. The feminists argue that dolls restrict women early in life to the role of mother, but Ginny was more an ego-surrogate for her little owner than a child image. Her image was not of a dependent little infant that needed continual mothering, for she was more an adventurous little girl who thrived on activity and needed a human owner to provide the necessary energy. If the little girl identified with the doll as a miniature version of herself, she must have been influenced by its physical properties. The Ginny doll, though very small and pretty, was virtually unbreakable and able to withstand years of active play. Those little girls who repeatedly heard myths of the 'weaker' sex must certainly have taken courage from their eight inch counterparts, both feminine and strong, both lovely and enduring."

And so, it is interesting to remember that Ginny was created by Mrs. Jennie Graves who was seeking independence, a woman who'd lost her husband and had a family to support and was thrown into the business world at a time when it was very difficult for women to succeed outside the home.

As Lia says it is not surprising that Ginny is the doll who may have liberated a generation of women.

GINNY AND AMERICAN CULTURE

When Dr. Robert Sargent goes to his classroom at Hofstra University, Ginny doll sometimes accompanies him. Or to be exact she is sometimes in his lectures. As Director of the American Studies Program one summer, the professor realized that Ginny was a contemporary artifact that reflected many aspects of American culture. After all his wife, Lia, had been collecting Ginnys for some time and had played with them as a child, so he couldn't help but notice the charm of the small dolls his wife collected.

"What struck me the most about the Ginny doll, states Dr. Sargent, "was the decision to make her in the image of a toddler, not a baby or an adult fashion doll. At the toddler stage the child is learning to walk, to explore the world on his or her own. Such a choice by Vogue, conscious or not, was inspired, as it is this stage of psychological development which is equivalent to the social and mythic image of Americans as innovators, inventors and explorers. America was the new land, the place where every man was free to discover him or herself as a unique person. Of course, there is no more unsettled land and there hasn't been for a hundred years or more. However, Americans still look for new worlds to conquer. They still hate to be stuck; they admire people who are mobile and take risks in order to discover new things just as the toddler does."

The professor also points out that Ginny was created and became popular at a time in our culture which was characterized by many moving from the city to the suburbs and also from farms to towns; this was the beginning of the shift from the extended family in which the individual had been largely bound by tradition and custom, and thrust into a new era - that of the nuclear family in which one has to define his or her own individual lifestyle. Vogue Dolls seemed to sense this need to choose an individual identity and establish a particular lifestyle by providing the wide range of clothing for Ginny. The little girl could explore a wide range of activities for differing lifestyles. Ginny was a very much played with doll as she served an important ego exploration function in a rapidly changing society, and she provided a way for little girls to deal with change and to try out new roles and adult identities.

As professor of English literature, Dr. Sargent has studied the psychological development of the protagonists in 19th century English novels, and became more aware of the numerous references to dolls in these novels and the significant role they often play in the growth of the characters. He states that he has also been struck by the unique nature of the Ginny doll and what it might suggest about American culture in the 1950's.

"The 19th century novels imply that a girl of those days had an intense relation-
ship with one doll and that doll was in some measure a means of overcoming a
temporary sense of isolation and loneliness"observed Dr. Sargent. "For example,
the doll appears as 'the solitary friend' of Esther Summerson in Charles Dickens'
BLEAK HOUSE; ' a faded, graven image, shabby as a miniature scarecrow' that helps
Jane Eyre to sleep in Charlotte Bronte's novel; and a 'fetish' punished by Maggie
Tolliver 'for all her misfortunes', in George Eliot's THE MILL ON THE FLOSS.

"Dolls probably continue to play this sort of role today; however, the nature of
the Ginny doll phenomena suggests that some change may have taken place. Ginny
was the first doll to be given her own family and was also the first with an
elaborate wardrobe and custom furniture. What has happened is that with the trend
set by Vogue several dolls came to replace one doll; a substitute family replaced
a substitute friend; a lavishly equipped and outfitted collection of dolls replaced one doll with few clothes and props. These changes might be traced to
several factors present in America in the 1950's. The emphasis of the times was
on family togetherness. However, the move from cities and rural areas to brand
new suburban communities made homeground unfamiliar and families became somewhat
separated from the traditions of the grandparents. World War II was over, the
Depression in the past; those who grew up with little might give much more to
their children. Mass production allowed more people to buy more. Thus, a family
of dolls like Ginny with elaborate outfits satisfied psychological and economic
needs. Though Ginny was a doll of her time, she is more also. Though mass produced, every single one that I have seen looks unique. Each has her own individu-
ality that is a mysterious combination of sculptured design, variation of wig
style and coloring. There is magic here that transcends hard plastic and mass
production and suggests that Ginny is the best of the old and the new as an expression of contemporary American culture. "

This pair of dolls dressed as
Pilgrims are an example of how
Ginny dolls reflect American
culture. Here are Priscilla
and John Alden from the series
of FROLICKING FABLES in 1952.
The matching garments are a
pale gray with white plastic
collars and cuffs. Her cap,
apron and shawl are organdy
and both have buckled black
leatherette shoes. He wears
a high black wool felt hat
and black belt.

GINNY'S FIRST SECRET

The only storybook ever written for little girls about the Ginny doll was GINNY'S FIRST SECRET, authored by Lee Kingman and illustrated by Hazel Hoecker. It was published by Phillips Publishers, Inc., of Newton, MA and sold for $2.95. The publishers are no longer in business and the book has become a collector's item. It was released in 1958, the year of Ginny doll's greatest heydey when 7,000,000 girls were loving and playing with her and over $10,000,000 worth of Ginny accessories were sold.

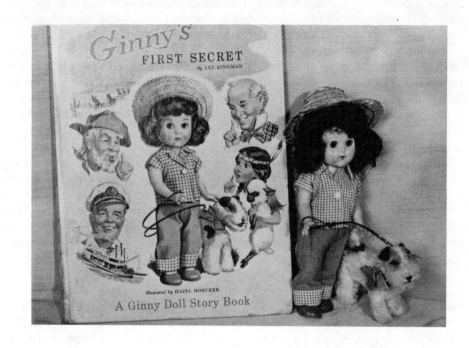

The dust jacket of the book proclaims that the author has skillfully captured the imagination of everyone for "the book not only carries a wealth of entertaining excitement and adventure but the message goes far beyond entertainment; it gives the young reader a truth to have, hold and apply in daily living".

As the story's heroine, Ginny travels, has exciting adventures, meets new friends and does learn a great truth. The book was written in a picaresque style somewhat reminiscent of DON QUIXOTE, dealing with a main character who roamed from place to place having myriad adventures. The plot centers around Ginny being told that the family is going to have to make a long move across country which makes her very unhappy. She is afraid that the new home will be the dullest, loneliest and saddest place in the whole world. Ginny is somehow separated from her parents in the process of moving and travels across country meeting many people and having various experiences along the way. Out west she makes friends with an old gold miner who tells her a secret. Everywhere her pup, Sparkie, the airedale, accompanies her. After spending the night in an old hotel in a ghost town where the hotel manager also tells her a secret, she boards a bus for the trip across Texas. Here she meets with a young Indian lass who shares a secret with her.
An aunt meets Ginny in New Orleans and from there she gets to ride on a Mississippi river boat where the captain tells her a special secret. Finally, the last stage of the trip is on an airplane and Ginny's family is there to meet her to take her to their new home, a big white house on the lake. Ginny decided that the new home is the greatest, happiest and nicest place in the whole world, and then she is able to put together the big secret and share it with everyone:

> "Open your heart -
> Open your mind -
> Look for the best,
> And that's what you'll find."

So, we see a facet of American culture when families were moving from the rural areas to the city or from the city to the suburbs. America was very much on the move in the 1950's as new job opportunities opened up sometimes many hundreds of miles away. In a way this marks the beginning of our affluent society. The book must have been very helpful to small children who had to undergo the experience of moving, which would have caused a great deal of anxiety. Through Ginny's experiences the young child could relate to her moving and perhaps better understand his or her own fears and anxieties.

Again in GINNY'S FIRST SECRET we see Ginny in the unisex role, ready for any adventure that befalls her. She is like a free little spirit that comes and goes and does what she wants to do.

LEE KINGMAN

Lee Kingman was commissioned by Phillips Publishers to do GINNY'S FIRST SECRET, the only book she has ever done on commision and, also, the only book she has ever written about a doll. However, Mrs. Kingman is the author of over 25 children's books and she also writes reviews of juvenile literature for several newspapers. She is currently editing books about art and illustration in the children's book field. She is married and the mother of two children, including a daughter who played with Ginny doll as a youngster. A graduate of Smith College, Mrs. Kingman was formerly an editor of young people's books for Houghton Mifflin Company and is now associated with Doubleday Press. She and her husband make their home in Massachusetts.

HAZEL HOECKER

Hazel Hoecker is a graduate of Washington University, the Chicago School of Fine Arts and the New York Art Students League. Originally from Connecticut, she resided on Cape Cod for a number of years. In the early 1950's she was associated with an unusual and romantic studio, a Mississippi river boat achored on the waterfront at St. Louis. This experience provided ideal material for several of the illustrations in GINNY'S FIRST SECRET. Children's books have been of special interest to Miss Hoecker and she was a free lance artist in New York for a number of years specializing in children's books. Now retired to Florida, she is a doll maker and creates colorful characters representing various regions of the country.

THE WOMAN BEHIND THE DOLL - MRS. JENNIE H. GRAVES

The Ginny Doll Story would never have become a reality had it not been for a very unusual, talented and creative lady who loved dolls and doll clothes - Mrs. Jennie Graves.

Born in Somerville, Massachusetts, on May 14, 1890, Jennie was the daughter of Franklin Adler and Anne Fuller (of the Fuller Brush Company family). During her childhood at the turn of the century she delighted in sewing for her dolls by gathering up scraps of material left by the seamstress who came to the house to sew for the family. At about the age of nine, two of her little cousins were visiting and told her about having to move to Boston and they were preparing to take their beloved china dolls with them. In honor of the occasion, Jennie made two special Red Riding Hood outfits for the dolls and thus, this warm act of generosity marked the earliest beginnings of her creative interest in dolls.

Jennie's father died when she was 15 years old and as the oldest of four children it was necessary for her to help support the family. She had graduated from Somerville High School and Fisher Business College but job opportunities for young girls were scarce and she took the first opening she could find in a wholesale fish company in Boston. It paid $8.00 a week with few holidays off and no paid vacation. After a year, her luck turned and she found work in a ladies' lingerie shop in Boston. Amidst new surroundings of luxurious drapes, velvet carpets and fine lace curtains she found her first real inspiration and enthusiasm for dolls. Her salary was $15.00 a week, which was considered top at the time. After five years she resigned to be married at the age of 21 and became the bride of Mr. William H. Graves on June 28, 1913. Three children were born and Mrs. Graves was kept busy sewing for them and creating chic outfits for her two daughters' dolls and those of neighbor children. Her reputation spread and a friend asked her to dress some dolls for a church bazaar and she returned for more several times. Jennie's charitable instincts were somewhat shocked when she accidentally found the dolls on sale at a large department store in Boston. She then decided that if her friend could sell the dolls there was no reason she couldn't sell them herself.

So, her imagination, drive and ambition coupled with courage and perseverance led her to start her own small enterprise, The Vogue Doll Shoppe in 1922. She began with three large German bisque dolls and dressed them in outfits similar to ones she had designed for her daughters. A buyer bought the dolls immediately and gave her an order for more. Soon card tables were put up in the kitchen which was her first workshop. She expanded to the basement and converted one of the bedrooms to a stock room. The garage was used for the shipping room with her son's wagon called into service to truck orders back and forth between the cellar and the garage. The neighbors began complaining about the express truck that stopped every· day and she had no alternative but to find manufacturing space elsewhere so she rented a store with rooms over it.

After six months the business had outgrown this space and with the assistance
of the Medford Chamber of Commerce an old WPA Building with 4,000 square feet
of floor space was leased and an additional 4,000 square feet the next year.
This location served for several years but after that there were two more
moves and by 1951 two plants were in operation, one in Medford and another
in Malden.

About the mid 1930's the name was changed to Vogue Dolls (and later to Vogue
Dolls, Inc.) and the plant employed some 50 women, mostly neighbors and friends
to sew the garments and dress the dolls. Mrs. Graves lost her husband pre-
maturely in 1939 and turned her attention to expanding the business to support
her children, who were still in school. The company made clothes for the popular
Patsy dolls as well as dressing fine imported German bisque dolls. Some of
these larger ones had gorgeous outfits that retailed for $50.00 and $75.00.
With World War II, it became increasingly difficult to import the German dolls
and so it was imperative to find an American source. Some of these were composition dolls obtained from the Arranbee Doll Company. Later Vogue had their
own doll designed which eventually became GINNY, named after Mrs. Graves' eld-
est daughter, Virginia.

The Ginny Doll scored the first important merchandising triumph for Vogue. Jennie
Graves decided to attack the market with every promotional scheme at her command.
She made arrangements with five of the most important department stores between
Boston and Washington to stage an all-out Vogue Doll promotion. There were big
scale newspaper ads, storewide sales advertising and window displays. With this
full scale promotion, enthusiasm for the dolls was generated as never before
known and all five stores sold out their stock in a few hours and sent in new
orders.

Jennie Graves became a celebrity in the Doll World and was in demand as a speaker
for large audiences, radio shows and television appearances. She traveled everywhere to promote her dolls. As the dynamic Mrs. Graves hustled and bustled around
between her office and all points, no one would think she had time for a hobby but
she was quite a connoisseur of milady's millinery. The exact number of chapeaux
she had stacked away was never fully known but she had them in all sizes and
shapes. However, her favorite ones were the large cartwheel variety, all frothy
with feathers and flowers. The Vogue doll lady, in spite of being a famous woman
industrialist, was still a warm-hearted, down to earth feminine woman and a credit
to womankind. She had a genuine love of poeple and was always very much like a
mother to all her employees. In her travels around the country she always managed
to find a little time form her busy schedule for a shopping spree and usually returned with at least one new hat. She was a petticoat boss who had a lot on her
mind besides that frilly chapeaux. Her special love of hats is reflected in the
eye-catching outfits of her dolls as most of them had beguiling little hats or bonnets that matched or complimented their costumes.

The excess profits tax at that time had no provision for a small business which
rapidly and successfully expanded with the result that the tax rate on Vogue Dolls
had jumped in five years from 21% to 70% in 1952. Mrs. Graves made a dramatic
presentation that had a strong impact on the House Ways and Means Committee. The
congressmen were impressed. They had listened to the tax lawyers drone on for weeks
with statistics on the subject but Mrs. Graves doll babies dramatized for them the
plight of the small business caught in the excess profits tax squeeze. One of the
representatives remarked that "it is conclusive in my mind against any extension of the
excess profits tax". Rep. Goodwin who comes from Mrs. Graves' hometown, also
agreed and he said that Massachusetts was proud of her, that her case was typical
of thousands of small businesses whose success was nipped by the profits tax.

Many awards and honors were bestowed on Mrs. Graves. The Boston Business and Professional Womans Club named her the Woman of Achievement for 1956. She was selected as Woman of the Week by the New York Journal American and her biography appeared in Who's Who of American Women.

After her retirement at age 70 in 1960 to Falmouth, Massachusetts, she remained as chairman of the board of her company. She was active in many community activities and civic affairs and had a keen interest in philanthropic projects. She launched the Nimble Thimbles, a group of 15 older women who liked to sew and this group raised over $18,000 for the Falmouth Hospital. The group has continued in memory of Mrs. Graves and have to date contributed approximately $35,000 to the hospital. Mrs. Graves passed away at the age of 81 in 1971. Hers was truly an American success story, a woman before her time who rose to the top in her chosen field from sheer determination, perseverance and faith in her product.

Miss Jennie Adler became the bride of Mr. William H. Graves on June 28, 1913 and this is her wedding portrait.

The picture very graphically depicts Mrs. Graves' love of hats and this one was a special favorite of hers.

Photo courtesy of Mrs. Virginia Graves Carlson, daugher of Mrs. Graves for whom the Ginny doll was named.

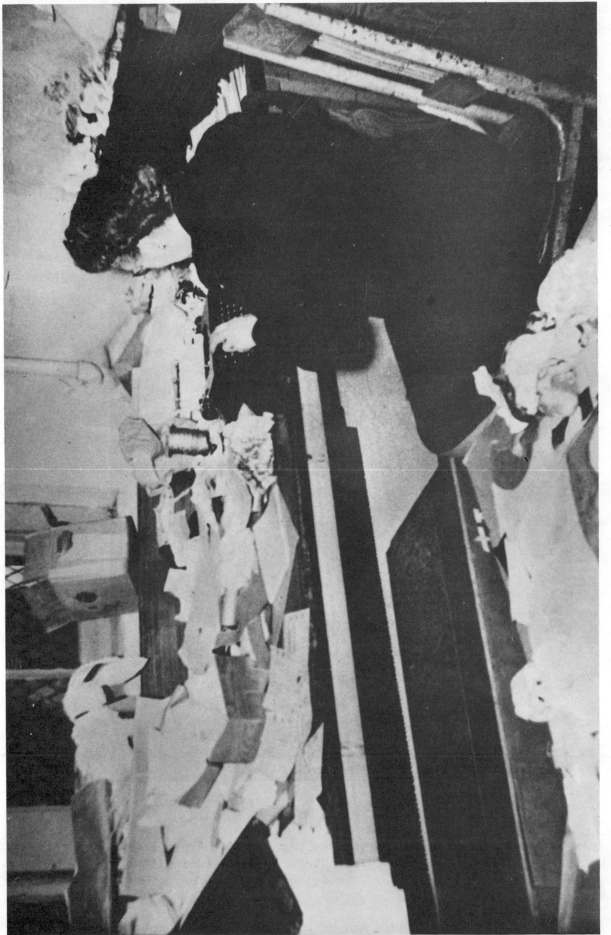

Medford, MA 1951. Vogue had just moved into their Ship Avenue quarters when this 'famous' photo of Mrs. Graves was taken. Note the big, old and well-worn desk with typewriter, file box to the left, jammed full of data, piles of papers everywhere, a beat up old kitchen chair, and in the foreground dolls with **patterns and cost information**. The movers were still 'moving in' and reportedly, Mrs. Graves **didn't** stop for anything!

Vogue photo

This is the Virginia Graves Carlson's favorite photograph of her
mother, Mrs. Jennie H. Graves. This picture was taken in 1954 when
Mrs. Graves was 64 years old.   Note, another one of Mrs. Graves'
stylish hats.

All photographs of Mrs. Graves and Mrs. Carlson are from the Graves-
Carlson family albums; courtesy of Virginia Graves Carlson.

October, 1957. Mrs. Jennie Graves looks over an exhibit of Ginny dolls
in various costumes that were produced that year. Ginny's little sister,
Ginnette, can be seen at the left of the photograph.   Vogue photo

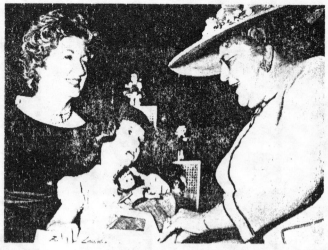

In 1955 Jennie Graves made an extended business trip out to the West Coast where she met many movie celebrities and their children. Above left she is shown with the Pat O'Brien family and their daughter Bridgid with Ginny. Other Hollywood notables that she visited, whose children were all Ginny fans include: the Ronald Regans and daughter, Patricia Ann; the Jack Wrathers (Bonita Granville) and their daughter, Linda; and the Wendell Coreys and children, Jennifer, Robin and Bonnie. Ginny was reported irrestible to many other daughters of movie stars including Dana Andrews,MacDonald Carey, Robert Cummings, Dennis Day, Bob Hope, Frank Sinatra, Maureen O'Sullivan, Jayne Mansfield, Ken Murray, Joan Bennet, James Mason and Esther Williams. While out west, Mrs. Graves appeared on the CBS television production, "Panorama Pacific", another television network program, "Crosby's Calling" and granted radio and press interviews including foreign news services. In the photo to the right, Mrs. Graves is presenting a Jill doll to television personality Maggi Mc Nellis and her daughter, Meg, 1957.

In 1959, Mrs. Graves was looking over a Ginny that was going to the Moscow exhibition of dolls and toys from the U. S. that were representative of American culture.

Vogue photo

THE ORIGINAL GINNY - Mrs. Virginia Graves Carlson

The first, real alive Ginny was Jennie Graves' oldest daughter, Virginia. As a young girl in her teens, Virginia took considerable interest in her mother's business and often worked during school vacations and through the summer in the Vogue plant. She was jack of all trades, helping in the shipping room, dressing and wigging dolls, even working on the books. Her mother was still designing the outfits in those days, but after Virginia graduated from the Modern School of Design in Boston, she officially joined the company in 1945 as the designer and remained in this position for over 20 years.

The original Ginny, Mrs. Virginia Graves Carlson for whom the Ginny doll was named.

Virginia was born in Somerville, Massachusetts, March 28, 1919. She married Stanley G. Carlson of Brockton, MA in 1954 but continued her career with Vogue. She was responsible for all the fashions for the entire Vogue line, including all the Ginny Doll Family as well as the larger dolls that were introduced over the years. Of course, there were more outfits produced for Ginny than any other doll. For a number of years, Vogue came out with 100 new costumes for Ginny every year. There were at least a dozen different bridal outfits, a great variety of nursery rhyme and foreign costumes. Virginia always agreed with her mother that dolls should look like American children and be dressed like them. Often she would get ideas from seeing children at play or going to school. Mother and daughter would pore over fashion trends in magazines including trade journals such as "Women's Wear Daily". Clothes for special events or those of far away places were always thoroughly researched in the library. Virginia always kept up to date on fashion trends for young folks so that her little foster children would have the latest in current styles. She especially liked to design the fancy party frocks for the dolls.

Virginia Carlson worked by the draping of material method; that is placing the fabric directly on the doll. From the draped figure she made an exact pattern from paper. This was then sent to the die maker and a steel cutting die was made, a duplicate of the original pattern. The dies then stamped the pattern piece on material sometimes cutting as many as four dozen at a time. She often would stay up all night in order to finish a new creation.

It seemed only fitting when the time came to name the little eight inch doll that it should carry the name of the designer of all her clothes, for it was Virginia Graves Carlson who created all the hundreds of little garments from the birth of Ginny doll through her heyday of the 1950's and beyond. It seems more than coincidence that Virginia's young girl picture even looked like a Ginny doll; the same little round face, sparkling eyes, button nose and similar hair style.

Young Miss Virginia Graves about age three in Sommerville, Massachusetts. Note the close resemblance to Ginny doll.

The story of how the Ginny doll was named is interesting. The first hard plastic eight inch dolls had various girls' names but the company felt that one name for the same doll would help in promotion. There were many buyers for stores and toy shops all over the country and many made suggestions for names in honor of their own daughter or a favorite female. Mrs. Graves put an end to all the discussion by declaring emphatically and with finality that the doll would be named for her own daughter, Ginny.

Virginia Carlson retired in 1966 to Falmouth to care for her mother. Nowadays, Virginia occupies her time with many civic and philanthropic endeavors, as well as a number of hobbies. She loves and appreciates good music. She retains an interest in dolls and still has a minor collection of Ginnys, just a few that represent her quarter century of work. She has some antique doll furniture such as cribs, cradles and high chairs and all are occupied by Vogue's life size Baby Dears attired in antique baby clothes. She also collects miniatures and is interested in many types of handicrafts. An outdoor lover and interested in conservation, one of Virginia's special loves is gardening. Her home is full of flourishing plants and gives evidence of a very green thumb. She has won blue ribbons and tri-color ribbons for the best in the show in a flower show of the Massachusetts Federation of Garden Clubs. She is listed in Who's Who of American Women. Now being developed as a special beauty spot in the community through the Historical Society and the Falmouth Garden Club is a Memorial Park. Mrs. Carlson spends a good deal of time watering, planting and supervising in memory of her husband who died in 1973.

It is certainly clear that Virginia Graves Carlson possesses many of the same characteristics that typified her mother, a genuine wholesomeness, down to earth quality with a love of people, a happy disposition and a positive, cheerful outlook on life. She has many fond memories of working together so happily with her mother in something they both shared and loved and she can always look back on the many delightful years they had together. And Virginia carried on her mother's ideals in fine workmanship and quality merchandise in producing a doll and her accessories that are the delight of collectors now and in the years to come.

May, 1950, Medford, Massachusetts: Mrs. Jennie H. Graves and her daughter, Miss Virginia Graves can't think of a woman who ever closes her eyes to dolls. Leaders in the doll industry, the mother-daughter team still effervesce over their chicly dressed dolls. As designer, Virginia concocts ensembles for the dolls that might well put the best dressed women of the year to shame. Together mother and daughter dream up costumes so smart that, with appropriate hairdos, each Ginny takes on a distinctive personality all her own. Each year, the team pore over fashion trends so that their 'foster children' will be without peer in their orginal clothes.

Mrs. Virginia Graves Carlson, left, and her mother, Mrs. Jennie H. Graves, are shown in this 1956 photo standing beside an array of Ginny dolls in outfits that were offered that year. Mother and daughter compare notes on the dolls clothes and are already busy dreaming up new togs to be re-designed the following year.

VOGUE - A COTTAGE INDUSTRY

Vogue Dolls has always been in the business of dressing dolls as they sub-contracted actual production of the dolls themselves. At first, friends and neighbors sewed the garments and later more dressmakers were hired as the industry grew. In the 1950's there were at least 500 home sewers and at the peak years in the late 50's there were about 800 women sewing at home besides several hundred employees at the plant. The home sewers were recruited from four states: Maine, New Hampshire, Vermont and, of course, Massachusetts, where the main plant was located.

JENNIE DAVIS

Jennie Davis worked as a home sewer for Vogue from 1956-58 working in her home in New Hampshire. She states that she would receive the outfits all cut out in the mail, four dozen at a time. Directions were included and also a sample of the garment already made up to go by. She then returned the finished outfits by mail along with the samples, trim, labels, etc. Jennie says, "it was fun sewing them as there were so many different styles and I wish I could do it again".

PHYLLIS CLARK

Another home sewer was Phyllis Clark, now a resident of California. She lived in Medford, MA at the time, about 1947, when she worked for Vogue. She would go to the plant to pick up the work and remembers feeling just flabbergasted when she was given the box of cut out garments to be made. Each piece was in a stack about two inches high and there were separate piles for the skirts, blouses and other pieces. One had to know their sewing machine very well and be able to use all the attachments, she recalls. "You would do the same operation on each piece, assembly line fashion. I just loved doing it and was sorry when we moved away". At that time no tags were being sewed into the garments.

ORIGINAL VOGUE PATTERNS

SKATING OUTFIT: Vogue used red and white dotted cotton with red lining. Red rick rack on the neck and sleeves and red dotted panties. Use 1/4 seams.

Seam shoulders, sew rick rack on sleeves close to the edge, also around the neck. Turn rick rack under and stitch. Sew underarm and side seams.

Hem back narrowly and stitch. Sew skirt and lining, right sides together except at waist. Turn and press. Gather skirt to fit top. Sew skirt to top. Top stitch around waist with seam pressed up. Sew on snap.

Panties: Use a piece of material 3"x8". Hem one long side with 1/4" hem. Start elastic at one end and stretch to other end as you sew. Place elastic on top of panties, fold cloth over 1/2". Stretch elastic as you sew but don't sew elastic. Close back seam. Match center front to center back right sides out. Sew a 1/2" line to form the pseudo crotch.

COWGIRL OUTFIT: Vogue used a dark blue with black vest and cuff with silver trim. Use 1/4" seams. Utilize skirt pattern from skating outfit. Do not cut on fold.

Lay bodice down right side up. Place black vest on bodice right side up. Sew braid into black edge across vest. Sew silver rick rack along neck and back edge. Turn rick rack under and stitch down.

Place black cuff on wrong side of sleeve and stitch across. Turn cuff back to right side of sleeve and sew on trim. Sew sleeves to bodice. Sew sleeve and side seams.

Sew fringe on bottom of skirt. Pleat 1/4" of each side to center front. Hem back edges and sew to bodice. Close skirt about 1 1/2" including the fringe. Sew on hook and eye.

Panties: Same as for skating outfit. Use silver rick rack on leg edges before sewing crotch.

These two patterns courtesy of Jennie Davis, former Vogue home sewer.

DRESS: Vogue used red or blue velvet for the bodice and white organdy for the skirt.

Turn sleeve edge in and stitch. Hem backs of neck with narrow hem. Fold under hem of neck in the front. Tack two small artificial flowers at two corners in front at Xs. Tack stem under at neck hem. Hem backs of bodice.

Stitch ribbon to right side of skirt along hem line. Embroider flower and leaves in red and green in three places along hemline. Hem back seams. Gather skirt.

Sew skirt to bodice. Sew back seam to top of ribbon. Close with one hook and eye at the waist.

KIMONA: Sew loop fringe along sleeve edges. Fold under and stitch. Sew underarm seams. Sew loop fringe around complete edge, starting at back neck edge. Fold under and stitch.

PINAFORE: Gather lace fairly full and assemble to shoulder strap by sewing lace to one side of strap, right sides together. Then fold strap on fold line and fold back seam line. Stitch.

Turn waistband in 1/8" each end and press in half lenthwise. Stitch straps to band at notches to form yoke so lace just meets underarm.

Turn up hem to right sides on notches, press and stitch lace flat on top of raw edge of hem, inserting one flower 1 1/2" from center front of skirt. Stitch other edge of lace, inserting flower 1 1/2" from C.F. Sew another piece of lace turned around and touching first row of lace.

Turn back placket of skirt and stitch entire length. Gather top. Stitch and yoke together. Sew hook and eye at waist. Seam back of skirt 1" only.

COAT AND HAT: Sew underarm seams, attach bodice to skirt. Sew tiny flowers at back near underarm. Add tiny rick rack as shown.

Sew brim to bonnet back, matching notches. Add ribbon ties.

Above patterns, dress and kimona courtesy of Phyllis Clark, former Vogue home sewer.

Art work on patterns by Marge Maginnis

OTHER PATTERNS FOR GINNY

There were, of course, a number of commercial patterns over the years that were designed especially for Ginny. Although no longer available over the counter in stores, they can still be obtained through collectors, found at doll shows, occasionally at flea markets, etc. There are doll collectors, also, who specialize in reproduction of these patterns. By diligent searching one can usually find these patterns in time.

Again, for a point of reference, we list here some of the known patterns for Ginny that were produced mostly in the 1950's; exact date when known is given below:
Anne Adams #193
Alice Brooks #1971 and 7229
Butterick #7972
McCall #1898, 1965 (1956), 2057 (1958), 2084, 2150 (1957), 2195, 8295 (1966)
Simplicity #1372, 1809, 2294

SKATING OUTFIT

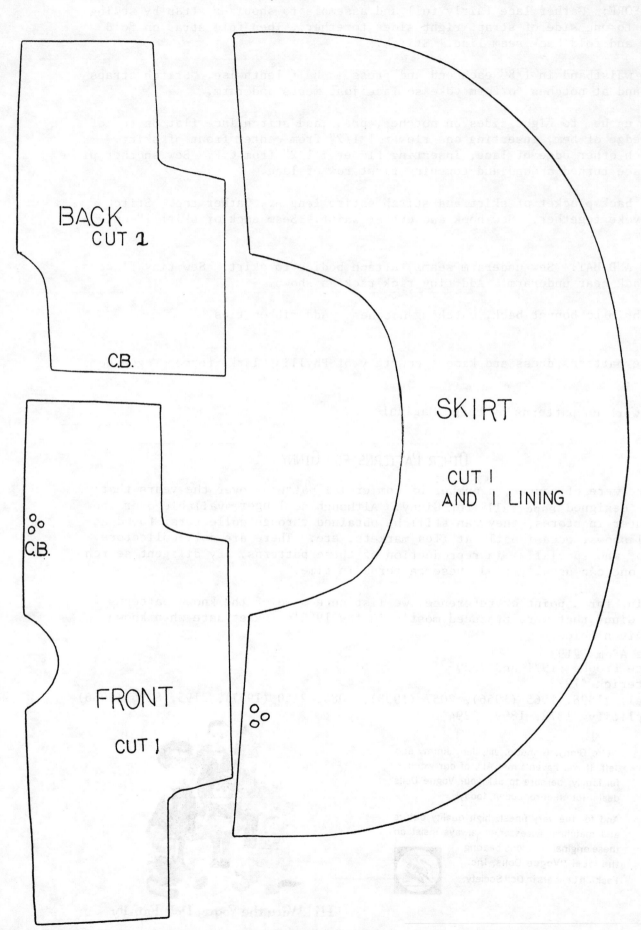

BACK
CUT 1

C.B.

SKIRT

CUT 1
AND 1 LINING

C.B.

FRONT

CUT 1

DRESS

COWGIRL SUIT

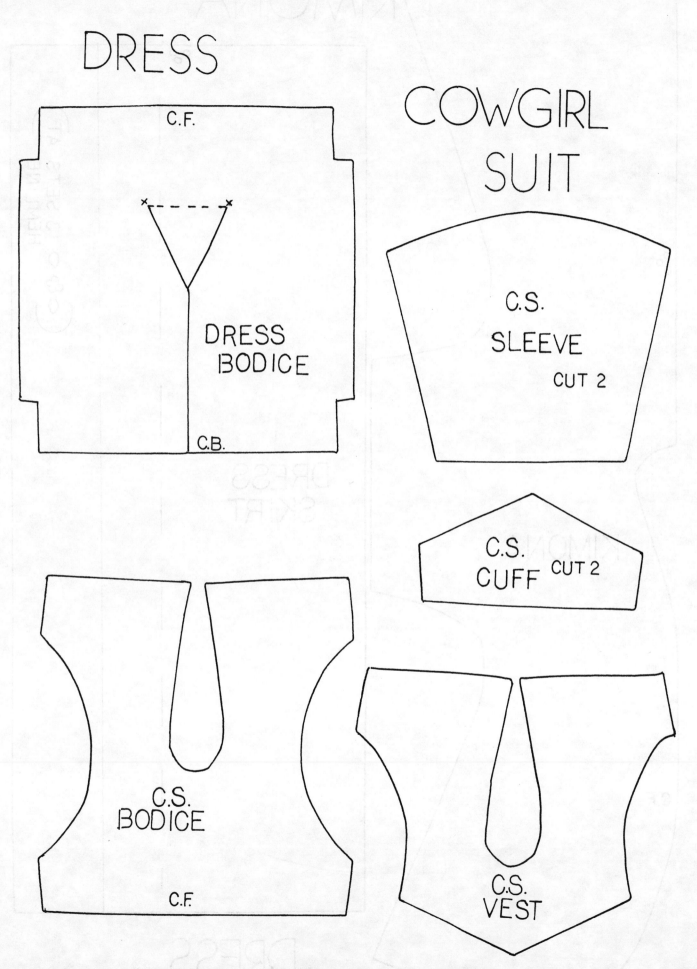

C.F.

DRESS BODICE

C.B.

C.S. SLEEVE
CUT 2

C.S. CUFF CUT 2

C.S. BODICE

C.F.

C.S. VEST

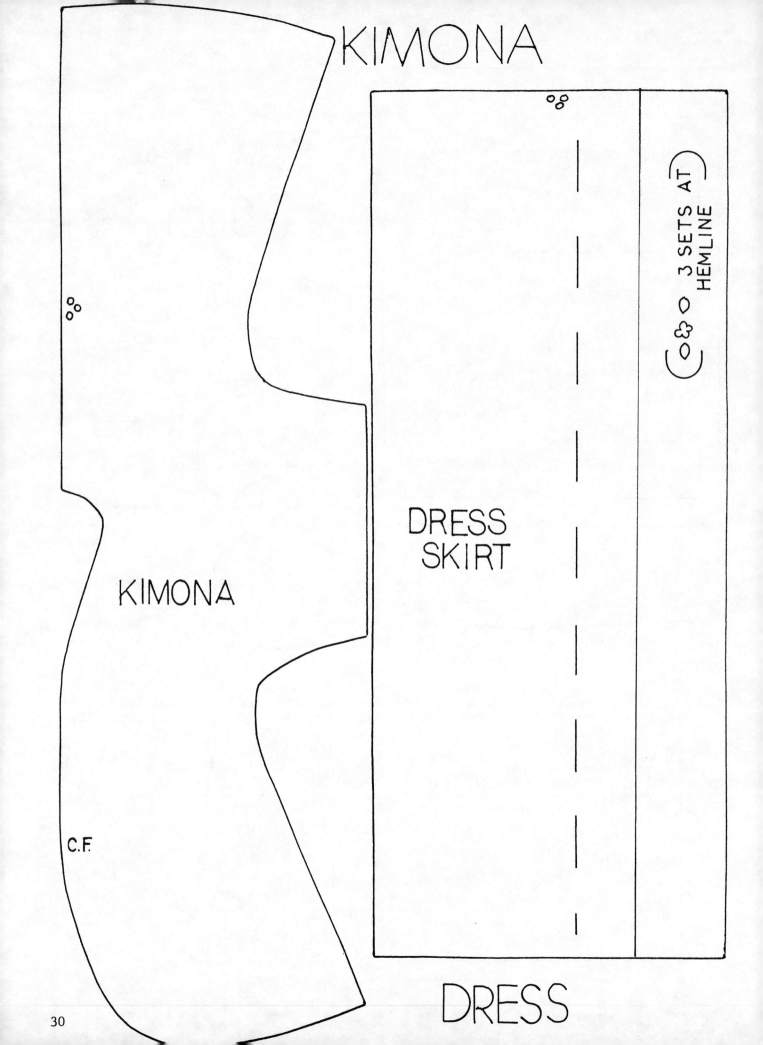

KIMONA

KIMONA

C.F.

DRESS
SKIRT

3 SETS AT
HEMLINE

DRESS

30

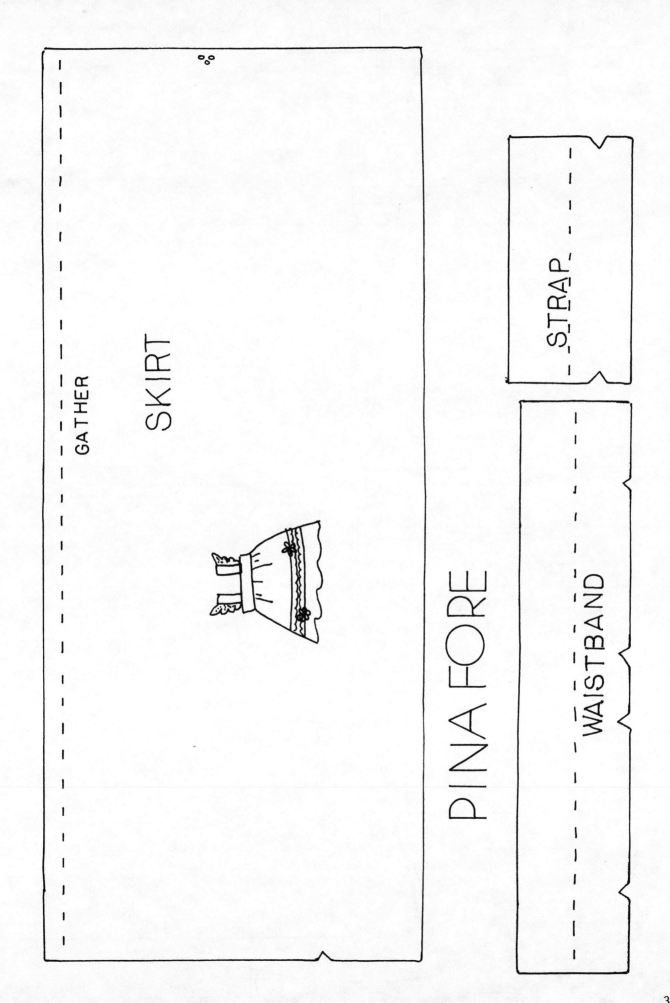

GATHER

SKIRT

PINA FORE

STRAP

WAISTBAND

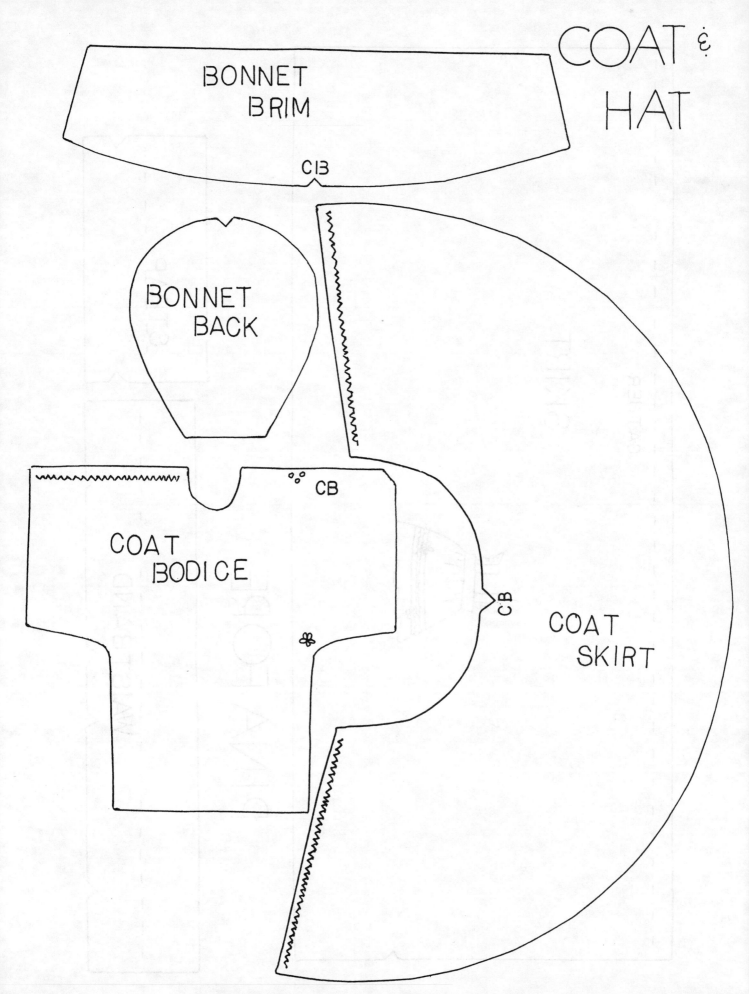

COAT &
HAT

BONNET
BRIM

CB

BONNET
BACK

CB

COAT
BODICE

CB

COAT
SKIRT

VOGUE CLOTHING LABELS

Research on 1950's labels courtesy of Ann Bergin

1930's.   Earliest known label used, probably only in clothes for JUST ME dolls. Vogue is written in yellow gold on white cotton and is sewed folded in the outfit.

1945-46. This is white cotton twill with blue lettering. It is folded in half and sewed into garment on the outside back in most clothes. Used with compostion dolls.

Later 1940's. Tag is white cotton with white letters on a blue background, sewed on outside back of outfit, some-time folded. Used on composition and first hard plastics. There seemed to be a period of time when no labels were used but perhaps small round paper tags appeared on the front of the costume.

1951. White rayon label with blue lettering seems to have been mostly folded and sewed into the garment on the out-side back. These were used with the #3 Ginnys who still had the mohair wigs.

1952. Blue print on white rayon ribbon appeared both sewed into the outside and inside of back of outfit. This was used on #3 Ginnys with lambskin and dynel wigs.

1953. Blue print on white rayon ribbon sewed inside back of garment. The was used on #3 Ginnys with dynel wigs.

1954-56. Black print on white rayon ribbon sewed inside back of dress. Used with #4 Ginnys.

1957 - mid 60's. Blue print on white cotton. This tag was sewed inside back of outfits on Ginnys #5, 6 and 7.

1966. Blue lettering on white cotton. Label was sewed inside back garments that Ginny #8 wore. This was the last label used on dolls made in U.S. and were used until pro-duction of Ginny ceased in this country.

1972. Dark green ink is used on a heavy white paper label sewed inside of skirt. These appear only on the #9 Ginny, made in Hong Kong.

Art work, courtesy of Marge Maginnis

Labels are shown actual size

This information is presented as a point of reference and is to be used only as an approximate guide for dates of the garments. There is considerable overlapping,so please keep this in mind. This might be explained by the fact that at the peak years of production, Vogue had 800 some home sewers at work making the garments. Naturally each home sewer would use up her supply on hand. According to Virginia Carlson there was no particular rhyme or reason for the changes in labels other than perhaps economic or aesthetic. They were redesigned whenever someone in the company got inspired with a new idea,and were not intended to signify the year the outfit was manufactured.

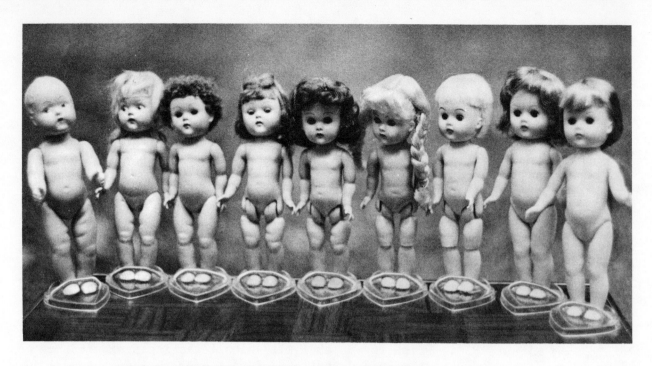

HOW TO DATE AND IDENTIFY YOUR GINNY DOLL

Pardon us bathing beauties: We're Ginnys and we want to show you how our molds and features have changed through the years. Now read about us from left to right:

1. 1937-1947 8" TODDLES or composition Ginnys. Early straight arm ones were marked VOGUE on back of shoulders (some were impressed R & B). Later bent armed ones were marked VOGUE on back of head and DOLL CO. on back of torso. This is a chubby toddler doll whose features were not well-defined; had molded hair with mohair wigs on some; eyes were painted blue and looked to the right; head, arms and legs all moved.

2. 1948-1950 First 8" hard plastic Ginny with painted eyes, molded hair with mohair wig. Dolls were marked VOGUE on head and VOGUE DOLL on back of torso.

3. 1950-1953 Moving eyes were added with painted lashes. In 1950 there was overlapping with #2. VOGUE was marked on head and VOGUE DOLL on back. Doll had straight legs, dynel foundation wigs with the poodle cut offered in 1952 only.

4. 1954 Walking mechanism added; still had painted lashes. GINNY marked on back and VOGUE DOLLS, INC., PAT. PEND. MADE IN U.S.A.

5. 1955 Plastic eyelashes were added. Marked VOGUE on head and on back was: GINNY VOGUE DOLLS, INC. PAT. NO. 2687594 Made in U.S.A.

6. 1957 Bending knees were added and marked same as above. There was some overlapping this year with #5.

7. 1963 Soft vinyl head with rooted hair was added to the hard plastic body. Head was marked GINNY, back was also marked GINNY VOGUE DOLLS, INC. PAT. NO. 2687594.

8. 1965 All vinyl plastic doll; straight legs, non-walker. Head marked GINNY, body marked GINNY, VOGUE DOLLS, INC. This is the last Ginny made in U.S.A.

9. 1972 Hong Kong Ginny, same mold as 1965 but head marked GINNY and back marked VOGUE DOLLS 1972 Made in Hong Kong.

10. 1977 Not pictured but shown on pages 146-150. Completely redesigned Ginny and made in Hong Kong. All dolls up to 1983 were from this mold. It is marked "Ginny Vogue Dolls, 1977".

REJUVENATING GINNY

Many readers will be looking for information on how to rejuvenate their Ginny doll. Ginny was a very much beloved and played with doll and is more often found in this condition than excellent or mint. Much can be done to help her look better. I am not an expert on this topic by any means, but perhaps I can offer a few suggestions and hints that I have found especially helpful and share them.

Sometimes just a few touches can make a big difference in improving the doll's appearance. Messy hair is about the worst offender. Try brushing it out with an old toothbrush or a wire bristled brush such as one used on suede shoes. The latter is especially good for very tangled or matted hair. However, be cautious when working with mohair; about the only thing that can help here is a hatpin and the mohair must be combed through very gently. Some wigs have been applied with glue spilling around the edges. If you want to remove the wig entirely, try soaking it in hot water. This should work on most wigs, but, if not, apply nail polish remover carefully into the wig, making sure it does not get on the doll's painted features as it will remove them, too. The remains of the glue on the head can be removed by the nail polish remover. You will probably want to shampoo the wig before restyling. Your own shampoo can be used, detergent for dishes or woolite if the wig seems especially fragile. Then, try either your own creme rinse or a fabric softener. If you don't have doll curlers, try fashioning some out of soda straws; wet the hair, roll it and fasten with a bobby pin. Comb the hair out gently when dry; you may want to brush the ends over your little finger or a pencil for a final set. Then, to make sure it stays, try some of your own hair spray or wig spray. For long haired wigs that seem to be entirely unmanageable, try combing out the best way you can and then braid it or put into a pony tail. Try different kind of hair styles until you get the one that pleases you the most. Replacement wigs are available for dolls who need it and these can be styled.

Actually, I have not had much experience in refinishing dolls. I've been told that the Flo Plaque paints are excellent especially for the plastics. It is difficult to do the facial features and I think one needs to have some artistic talent to be succesful at this. Crazing on composition dolls can be minimized by rubbing oil paints into the fine lines. Mix the oil paints to match the dolls' finish and try it out first on the back of the doll to see if it matches correctly. For larger cracks or repairing lost fingers or toes, try wood putty or plaster of Paris, sand down and then paint over. For badly decomposed compositions, the whole doll needs to be sanded down and repainted. This is really a job for the experts, I feel, but you may want to try your own hand at it. Pale doll faces can be helped with your own lipstick and rouge, at least temporarily. A clear spray over this will help to set the finish. Car wax is very good to help clean and preserve composition dolls as it is not water based.

Non walking Ginnys can easily be restrung. There are special sizes of elastic bands available for restringing the head to the legs and a smaller size for the arms. Walking and the knee bending dolls are difficult to repair. To do an adequate job, the doll must be taken apart from the seams. This must be done by heat, such as dipping in boiling water. Then pry the two pieces of the doll apart; once inside, you can examine to see where the trouble lies, repair, then glue back together. If the walking mechanism seems to be working improperly, try pulling down on the leg, as it is on a spring, and see if you can get the metal piece back in the groove on the leg. For seams that have cracks, apply heat; you can actually dip the hard plastic into boiling water as this softens the plastic enough so that you can firmly press the two parts back together. For the difficult places, try using a fast acting glue along with the heat.

I recommend the Doll Hospitals for serious repair jobs. They are usually staffed with well trained people who know what they are doing and will be most happy to repair your doll so that she looks like new again.

GINNY'S ROOTS

We know that Vogue imported fine German bisque head dolls such as those from K*R in the 1920's and into the 1930's and one of these is of special significance. This is the small Armand Marseille doll known as JUST ME. These dolls are very daintily porportioned with a bisque head that swiveled on an all composition body with moving arms and legs. There was a variety of hair styles but most had curly mohair wigs done in a poodle style. Sleeping eyes sometimes glanced to the side which technically puts them in the Googlie classification of dolls. In 1931, according to an article in PLAYTHINGS Magazine, Vogue introduced a wardrobe trunk for their 8" JUST ME with several changes of clothing in it. A price list for 1932 lists a 10" JUST ME with curly wigs and closing eyes and more than a dozen items of clothing including sweater, pleated skirt and beret, a four piece linen ensemble, beach togs, pajamas, a dotted swiss dress with silk coat and bonnet as well as colored percale, dimity, striped boradcloth, figured batiste and pastel organdy frocks, all complete with bonnets. In addition to this 10" JUST ME, there was also the little 8" one knownas PEGGY JEAN and listed as little sister to JUST ME. She has six complete changes of clothing. Vogue continued to produce elaborate wardrobes with fine detailing on the clothes, very much like one would sew for a child; by 1937 JUST ME was available as an all composition doll. All the dolls were marked JUST ME/Registered/ Germany with numbers that seemed to vary: A 310/7/0 M; A 310/110/ M; or A 310/11/0 M.

Photo at right shows both sizes of JUST ME dolls about 1933 with their wardrobe trunks. (Old Vogue photo, courtesy of Virginia Carlson.)

Below is 8" JUST ME in original clothes. (Photo by Lia Sargent.)

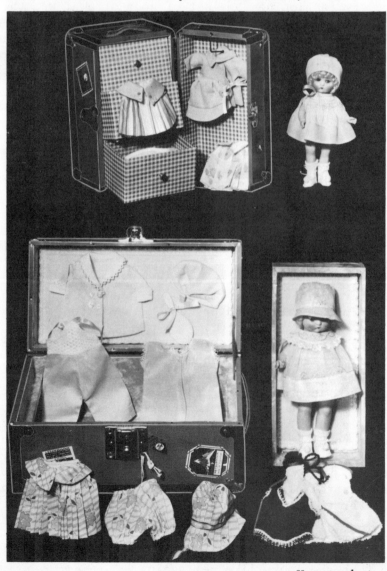

Vogue photo

When Mrs. Graves could no longer obtain the German dolls due to hostilities in Europe, she turned to American sources. She commissioned a sculptor to fashion a small toddler doll according to her specifications. She wanted one that would have the porportions of a real child; plump, round tummy, chubby legs and a winsome facial expression. Through the sculptor's hands and Mrs. Graves eyes and mind, there was produced a charming doll that was in some ways reminiscent of the smaller version of the JUST ME (Peggy Jean) doll. The new doll had a similar look with eyes glancing to the right, slightly curved right arm and plump body porportions. It was molded in composition which is composed of hyde glue, wood pulp (sawdust), resin and cornstarch. The name of this doll was TODDLES to the trade but it was never widely promoted to the public as such, and so it was commonly referred to as composition Ginny.

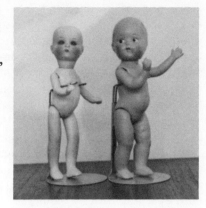

JUST ME (left) compared
with TODDLES (right)
Note similarities.
(Photo by Lia Sargent)

10" JUST ME with eyes glancing to the right and a human hair wig. Note chubby body and facial features similar to TODDLES

TODDLES (below) or composition Ginny. Note similarities to JUST ME; eyes glancing to the right, bent right arm and features of face.

BERNARD LIPFERT

The designer of Ginny and all her family was the German-born sculptor, Bernard
Lipfert, who spent nearly 70 of his 86 years dreaming of tiny painted faces.
Dolls were his passion and they were born in his basement out of clay and
plaster of Paris. Lipfert came from a family of toymakers and had worked for
Armand Marseille in Germany, so no wonder his American designed dolls, such
as Patsy and Ginny, bore a close resemblance to the German produced JUST ME.
Mr. Lipfert immigrated to this country in 1912 first settling in Minneapolis.
A year later he moved to the Queens, N. Y., where he was employed by the Hors-
man Doll Company. He soon was designing dolls for pratically every major
doll manufacturing firm in the country and over the years his name was associated with such famous personalities as Shirley Temple, Howdy Doody, Deanna
Durbin, Sonja Henie, Judy Garland, Pinocchio, all the Patsy dolls, Dionne
Quintuplets and Betsy McCall. In his later years, Mr. Lipfert made his
home in Westbury on Long Island, where his attic was stacked with doll heads
that he had been commissioned to do. He often initiated his own designs
which were adapted from the stacks of baby photographs and magazine clippings
that cluttered his workshop. His granddaughter was the model for the Baby
Coo doll. His formula seemed to be sure-fire; pretty dolls that looked real
but not too real. In the 1950's he designed the Toni doll with the permanent
wave that small girls loved so much, as well as Ginny whose popularity swept
the country. Toward the end of Lipfert's long life, he was somewhat dis-
illusioned because he didn't believe in gimmicks. To him a doll was to be
loved and cuddled and not mechanized. However, he went along with the changes
and designed faces on dolls with battery-operated voices and he copied the
likes of characters from television. Mr. Lipfert passed away in 1974 and
is survived by his wife, son and several grandchidren.

So, Ginny joins with the
other immortals of the doll
world in having been conceived
and designed by a famous
doll sculptor.

Bernard Lipfert sculpting
one of his dolls in his
studio about 1930. Note
photo of baby he used as
model and another finished
head below, center. In the
background are pictures of
babies on the wall which
he used as models.

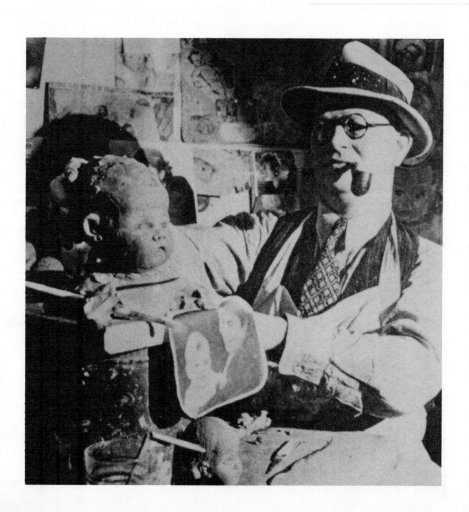

COMPOSITION GINNYS 1937-1947

The year of 1937 seems to mark the introduction of composition Ginny dolls by Vogue who also offered dolls in other types and sizes such as rubber and soft bodied dolls. This seems to be the last year, too, for the JUST ME dolls which were by that time being made of composition.

For some decades, collectors have referred to the early 8" Vogue doll as composition Ginny. However, an obscure salesman's price list reveals that they were listed as TODDLES to the trade but never widely promoted by that name so that it never became known to the public. Some of the composition dolls were obtained from the Arranbee Doll Company after Vogue no longer could import German dolls due to World War II. These were marked R & B on the back. Others, mainly early ones with the straight right arms were marked VOGUE on the back of the shoulders. Later ones with the bent right arms were marked VOGUE on back of the head and DOLL CO. on back of the torso. SUNSHINES or baby composition Ginnys were also impressed the same. SUNSHINES had baby curved legs, otherwise they were the same doll.

Most composition dolls are composed of similar materials such as wood flour or wood pulp (saw dust), Hyde glue, resin and cornstarch. Once out of the mold, the dolls were painted. The small 8" ones did not have well defined features. They all had blue eyes glancing to the right, molded hair which was painted in some models with mohair wigs added to others. The wigs were mostly blonde or brownette while a few character dolls like Indian, Pirate or Gypsy did have black hair. SUNSHINES all had molded hair, painted over while TODDLES had both painted hair and wigs.

During this decade, many different ensembles were created for the dolls, first by Mrs. Graves and later by her daughter, Miss Virginia Graves, who became Vogue's designer for all the dolls. The SUNSHINES or baby composition Ginnys were always attired in adorable baby clothes such as rompers and dresses with matching bonnets fashioned from fine cotton batiste, colored and white organdy and dimity material, some of them smocked and all with embroidery, lace and other colorful trims.

Probably the full extent of the dolls' wardrobes will never be completely known due to the passage of time and the lack of records but it is known that TODDLES came in various series such as NURSERY RHYME, FAIRY TALE, CHARACTER, FAR-AWAY PLACES and cunning little girl and boy togs. In addition there were some interesting groups presented during this time such as the CINDERELLA GROUP consisting of the FAIRY GODMOTHER, PRINCE CHARMING and CINDERELLA: MILITARY GROUP in honor of our American Servicemen and there were six in this group including UNCLE SAM, CAPTAIN, SAILOR, AVIATOR, NURSE and SOLDIER: The BRIDAL PARTY had the BRIDE, BRIDEGROOM, BRIDES MAID and MINISTER.

Separate clothes to fit these dolls were available in a flowered paper covered box with one drawer, size 7x5x3, and consisted of a party dress and bonnet, play dress and hat, farmerette overall, blouse, sunsuit and bonnet, kerchief, nightie, shoes, blouse, towel, soap, extra hat, hoe, rake and shovel.

FASHION LEADERS IN DOLL SOCIETY was coined by Mrs. Graves in 1943 as the slogan for her company, which became incorporated in 1945.

1942 group, from left and clockwise: FAR-AWAY LANDS series, Dutch girl and boy with real wooden shoes; Alpine girl and boy; American girl in pinafore. THESE ARE R& B marked dolls dressed by Vogue.

In keeping with the fast-moving American picture of 1943, these Vogue dolls were designed to express American-on-the-March to Victory! From far left and clockwise are the soldier, war nurse, sailor, American Indian and Miss America.

From left and clockwise: Miss Scotland from FAR-AWAY LANDS; others represent AMERICANA including Victory gardeners (boy and girl) and cowgirl and cowboy in matching outfits with rope. 1944.

World War II "MILITARY GROUP", 1943. At top and clockwise: Uncle Sam, Sailor, Soldier, Nurse, Aviator and Navy Captain. This is another example of the importance of Ginny dolls in depicting American history and social changes. Vogue photo

What the best dressed children wore during the World War II era, 1943. Follow these numbers from left to right starting with back row for description of outfits: 048 and 047 matching boy and girl in pastel jersey, caps and sweaters with doggie trim; 046 smocked dotted organdy dress and bonnet; 044 dotted organdy dress with embroidered roses and straw hat; 052 flowered dotted swiss with hamburg trim, pigtails are tied with large bows; 042 pink organdy with matching bonnet, hand embroidered roses and net trim; 050 flowered shadow organdy with full and gathered bonnet, lace and flower trims; 049 dotted organdy and bonnet with a panel of novelty trim as a focal point down the front of the frock. All the girls have panties attached to the dress and hooks and eyes are used in the back for closing. There are no labels and shoes are leatherette.

TODDLES: Vogue composition Ginnys from "CHARACHTER AND NURSERY RHYME" series. Above several dolls can easily be recognized by their dress such as; American Indian pair, Mistress Mary, Little Bo Peep, Cowboy, Jack and Jill while the other two are dressed as small girls. 1943. Dolls of this period are all wearing side snap leatherette shoes while shoes in photo below, dated 1947, all have leatherette pumps except for wooden shoes and skates. In bottom picture can be seen the Farmerette and Farmer at top and clockwise, Wee Willie Winkie, Gretel and Hansel, Red Riding Hood, Dutch pair and Ice skater.

Vogue photos

A STUDY IN COMPOSITION COUPLES. Above left and continue clockwise are a pair in Swiss costumes of green felt worn over white cotton **all in one piece shirts and** panties; Alpine couple are attired in orange felt with matching hats, and white cotton tops; English pair (below) wear brown cotton knit togs with England marked on bottom of shoes (note Vogue round paper sticker on boy's pants); the Russian twosome is colorfully attired in cotton and wool felt, his shapka (Russian hat) is black caracul. Russian girl, courtesy of Marge Meisinger. The dolls date about mid to late 1940's.

A STUDY IN MALE CHARACTERS. Above left and clockwise: ROBIN HOOD in green cotton tights with attached shirt, brown jerkin, felt hat and boots; POLICE-MAN (courtesy of Marge Meisinger) in dark blue suedecloth with his nightstick or billyclub; CLOWN in pink and blue taffeta suit with matching hat (courtesy of Eunice Peterson); and TYROLEAN wearing his lederhosen in heavy gray felt and Alpine hat.

CINDERELLA GROUP above, 1943. Fairy Godmother with wand is costumed in pale pink dotted swiss attached to a net petticoat and pantalets. There are long Edwardian pointed sleeves and her high pointed hat bespeaks the medieval era of this age old tale. Prince Charming is wearing pink cotton knit tights with attached white organdy shirt with lace jabot and over this is a weskit of printed pastel blue satin with matching hat. Cinderella is attired in light blue organdy with lace trim, attached underskirt and pantalets and she also wears the high conical shaped hat that matches her dress and there is a flowing veil of gilt edged white rayon. Below are two versions of Red Riding Hood; one on right is late 1940's and one on left is an R & B marked doll dressed by Vogue, date of which is possibly late 1930's.

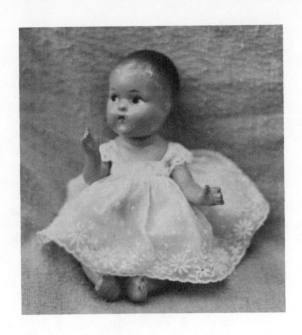

A STUDY IN SUNSHINES or BABY COMPOSTION GINNYS.   Above left and continuing clockwise; curved leg baby wears a pastel ninon gathered dress with embroidered trim and
attached slip (courtesy of Pat Spirek); bonnet and frock are pink organdy trimmed
in double rows of white baby rick rack with lace trimmed ruffled sleeves (courtesy
of Marge Meisinger); pink dimity has eyelet embroidery trim and satin ribbon sash;
three R & B marked curved leg babies are attired in cunning cotton frocks with
fancy trimmed matching bonnets. Dolls date early to mid 1940's.

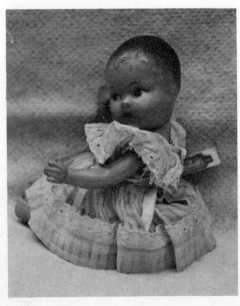

SOME INTERESTING COMPOSTION GINNYS. Above left and continuing clockwise: Southern Belle in long frock of flowered cotton with matching hat and nosegay; little girl in pink organdy with lace trim and matching bonnet; small boy in an all cotton knit outfit with matching socks and beanie hat; R & B marked doll dressed by Vogue in pale yellow cotton voile with bertha collar and bonnet - doll is wearing baby clothes but has straight legs. All dolls date from about early to mid 1940's.

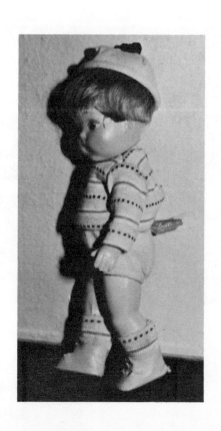

PAINTED EYE HARD PLASTICS

1948-50 were the only years that the painted eye hard plastic Ginnys were made. They were listed as just 'Toddlers' (not TODDLES) on salesmen's sheets, and are now commonly referred to as painted eye Ginnys. They have molded hair to which mohair wigs have been added usually in blonde and brown shades. These dolls are marked VOGUE on head and on the back of the torso VOGUE DOLL was also impressed.

In addition, there were eight inch painted eye hard plastic babies called CRIB CROWD with baby curved legs; they were the same doll, marked the same, the only difference being the bent baby legs. They wore rubber pants and had a bow in their ringlet styled wigs. Their adorable baby frocks were fashioned of dotted swiss, flocked organdy, ninon and cotton dimity with lace and bow trims.

Similar materials were used for the toddlers with straight legs. Fitted weekend cases were available for the dolls with changes of clothes, beach bag, face cloth, powder, nightie, bathrobe, slippers, soap, plastic comb and mirror.

1950 is the first year that the name GINNY ever appeared on any records. This was the name given to one doll wearing a colored velvet coat and beret with fur trim over a figured dress, outfit #8 3R. During this period dolls were given various girl's names according to the outfit they wore.

In 1948, Vogue was still making other size dolls such as a 14" all plastic doll and a 15" Velva wetting baby with washable real rubber skin and stuffed with foam latex. By 1950 the company was devoted exclusively to the production of eight inch dolls and the line was greatly expanded.

Vogue began a large scale promotion plan to sell dolls at times other than at Christmas with special numbers designed for other holidays including several for Valentine's Day, Easter and Springtime and Vacation along with their regular line of CHARACTER, NURSERY RHYME, SPORTS GROUP, EVENING and TWIN PLAYMATES, etc.

1950 is the year, too, of the famed ONE-HALF CENTURY GROUP consisting of seven dolls to represent every decade of the first half of our century plus Miss 2000. Virginia Graves did extensive research on period fashions in order to make the costumes authentically resemble the right decade in styles. Of special interest is the fact that Miss 1900 through Miss 1940 were all painted eyes while Miss 2000 had sleep eyes.

On the next several pages we reproduce various promotional sheets of the 1950 dolls, courtesy of Virginia Graves Carlson and used with permission.

FAIRY GODMOTHER   PRINCE   CINDERELLA

Happy Birthday to my own darling little Cinderella from her fairy Grandmother

A good Granny knows that a real little mother wants real dolls . . . with chubby real bodies, "real hair" to fix, and real clothes to take off and put on — even shoes. And a wise Grandma chooses unbreakable, all-plastic dolls that are completely washable.

So Granny's dolls for her darling are made by

Vogue Dolls, INC. MEDFORD, MASS.

51

VOGUE for Valentine's Day and *Easter*

DOLLS MEAN

More Profits for You!

Vogue Dolls, INC.
MEDFORD, MASS.

"For the dear little LADY-OF-YOUR-HEART"

NO. 2   NO. 1

All *Plastic* 8" DOLLS

Suggest that these dolls . . VOGUE Sweetheart and Queen of Hearts . . . are just the right gifts for that Valentine's Day surprise! Gals, young and old, will be delighted!!

Per doz.

VOGUE SWEETHEART
Valentine #1
With painted eyes $21.60
With moving eyes 22.50

QUEEN OF HEARTS
Valentine #2
With painted eyes $24.00
With moving eyes 25.20

IN THE SPRING
...A YOUNG GIRL'S FANCY TURNS TO
THOUGHTS OF LOVE, TOO!

And so here you see VOGUE'S "Springtime" and "Easter Parade" all dressed up as crisp and cute as can be! You can just imagine how pleased the one who receives them will be!! BE SURE YOU HAVE 'EM.

Per doz.

SPRINGTIME
Easter #21
With painted eyes $21.60
With moving eyes 22.50

EASTER PARADE
Easter #24
With painted eyes $24.00
With moving eyes 25.20

21   24

♥ PEP UP YOUR VALENTINE DISPLAY *with* ♥

All Plastic
8" DOLLS

They have amazingly perfect and fully-jointed bodies — lovely life-like mohair wigs.

No. 1 $21.60 per doz.

Right. Full circular skirt of shadow organdy — ribbon trim — red hairbow — "I love you" plastic locket.

No. 2 $24.00 per doz.

Left. Red taffeta dress — white organdy apron, lace trim. Heart hat — "I love you" plastic locket.

TENNIS   ROLLER SKATER   BEACH

a Present with a Future for the Birthday Child

What a wonderful surprise! Enchanting little playmates all ready to run out and romp in the garden! Brother, in overalls and straw hat, has a wheelbarrow — while Sister, in matching shorts and sunbonnet, helps out with a watering pot. Julie daintily tends the flowers in Rhumba-ruffled playsuit and bonnet, and carries her own watering pot. Each little charmer may be washed and dressed . . . All plastic, unbreakable and exquisitely constructed, these Vogue Dolls are the perfect playmates — and there's an extensive wardrobe available for them, outfits and accessories for every occasion.

IT'S VACATION!
AND WE'RE GOING PLACES ... IN STYLE

I'm off for a brisk set of Tennis (see my racquet?) . . . in shorts and blouse — with detachable skirt and a red sweater — and a sun visor, of course.

I Roller Skate like a ballerina . . . see my matching panties when I whirl . . . and my matching babushka too? Sometimes I go "boom!"

I think I'll go to the Beach . . . my play-suit has a lined Terry cloth cape and hood — and I carry my bathing suit in my wooden beach pail.

WE GO EVERYWHERE! We're VOGUE DOLLS! you can wash us — and our clothes . . . you can fix our hair . . . (we're all plastic and unbreakable, too!)

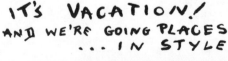

Vogue Dolls, INC.
MEDFORD, MASS.

Vogue Dolls, INC.
MEDFORD, MASS.

53

VOGUE DOLLS *Make* EXTRA
EASTER
PROFITS FOR YOUR STORE

Vogue Dolls, INC.
MEDFORD, MASS.

HELP THE EASTER BUNNY
WITH THESE NEW DOLLS!

NOTHING IS *Nicer* THAN GOOD DOLLS

All Plastic
8" DOLLS

8-6K — Colored organdy dress. Lacy bolero effect in yellow, orchid and all pastel shades. Colored straw hat (flowers and ribbon trim). Fluffy chick on arm **$24.00**

8-12K — Colored taffeta dress in yellow, orchid and all pastel shades. White organdy apron, lace trim. Lacy hat (ribbon trim). Fluffy chick on arm **$24.00**

NOTE: *Chicks appear on arm for Easter only. After Easter, these $24.00 numbers will have miniature handbags.*

SHOW THEM!
THEY'LL SELL!

8-12D — Colored taffeta dress. Net underskirt in yellow, orchid and all pastel shades. Satin hairbow. Fluffy chick on arm **$21.60**

8-10D — Full circular skirt of shadow organdy. Ribbon trim in yellow, orchid and all pastel shades. Satin hairbow. Fluffy chick on arm **$21.60**

NOTE: *Chicks appear on arm for Easter only.*

FITTED CASES — **8-30C** Complete wardrobes to fit 8" Vogue Dolls. Cases packed four to a carton. . . . **$27.00 doz.**
8-50C — Acetate case with doll and wardrobe (packed two to a carton) . . . . **$42.00 doz.**
DOLL STANDS for 8" Vogue Dolls (12 to a box) . . . . **$3.00 doz.**

1950 Dolls: Right is a special CRIB CROWD baby dressed as an Easter Bunny for promotion during the Easter season. The costume is pastel poodle cloth that matched the hair; note felt lined ears sewed into the wig and also the fluffy bunny tail.

Below, middle photo, are baby dolls promoted as follows: "A beautiful Baby to Baby . . .Welcome is the guest who remembers the youngest with a cuddly Baby Sister who will be the pet of the whole family." Dolls were named: 8-3L, Sally; 8-6L, Tootsy; and 8-1L, Betsy.

Bottom photo shows´ the individual outfits and separate accessories that were offered during 1950 by Vogue.

DON'T LET *the heat* CUT YOUR PROFITS

STOCK THE CRIB CROWD WITH CURVED BABY LEGS AND SPECIAL RINGLET WIGS

Per Dozen

8-3L—Col. Fig. and plain dimity dress with collar—Lace & Ribbon bows. $24.00

8-6L—Col. Satin Cape—Ninon dress. $27.00

8-1L—Col. & plain dimity romper, eyelet ruffling—Plastic toy. $21.60

(4 style dresses at $24.00. Order assorted).

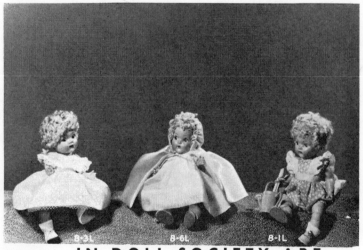

8-3L   8-6L   8-1L

FASHION LEADERS IN DOLL SOCIETY ARE READY FOR VACATIONS.

1800

NEW—Separate clothes individually boxed with acetate cover; include shoes, socks and accessories.

(Packed 6 per carton)

#1800 contains: Roller Skating outfit
Ice Skating outfit
Tennis outfit
3 different dresses (8-4K—
8-7K   8-11K) ....$13.80 doz.

#1810 contains: 6 assorted dresses 13.80 doz.

1950 CINDERELLA GROUP. The
Godmother's costume is
American beauty taffeta
and white dotted ninon
and she wears a conical
cap. The Prince has
blue cotton knit tights
with a satin vest and
hat. His shirt is lace
trimmed and there's a
feather in his cap. Cin-
derella's gown is white
sparkle ninon with blue
taffeta paniers and a
matching conical hat.
There is also a satin
covered pillow to carry
Cinderella's slipper.

1950 MISTRESS MARY. She is
wearing a light blue taffeta
dress with pantalets and a
staw hat with ribbon and
flower trim. There is net
trimming on her dress and
this serves to hold the
flowers from her garden at
the hemline of her dress.
Note VOGUE DOLL tag that is
attached to her wrist.

1950 BRIDAL GROUP. Groom
wears a full dress suit
of wool felt with flower
in buttonhole and a top
hat; bride's ensemble is
white brocaded satin with
a lily of the valley veil
and she is holding a prayer
book; the ring bearer's
costume is pink brocaded
satin suit with matching
beret and he carries a
heart shape pillow with
two rings. Missing in this
group is the bridesmaid who
had a flowered taffeta gown
with straw hat.

1950 ONE-HALF CENTURY GROUP. From upper
left and continue clockwise: MISS 1900
in a white dotted pink dimity long period
gown trimmed in lace and black ribbon with
a matching poke bonnet; MISS 1910 in a
calf length long waisted blue dotted swiss
dress, lace trimmed and with a sash and
large hairbow; MISS 1920 in a full skirted
white taffeta frock with blue velvet top
and puffed net sleeves and rosebud trim;
Miss 1930 in a yellow pin check broadcloth
outfit and a big hairbow (note her hair is
cut short in a Dutch bob); Miss 1940 has
a red flowered gingham dress with a straw
hat; Miss 1950 wears a red jersey sweater,
matching beret with a red plaid skirt and
she has long braids; Miss 2000 is attired
in a blue and red futuristic suit and a
hat with antenna. Note she has a special
ringlet wig and is a sleep eye doll while
other have painted eyes.

THE HEYDAYS - 1950's

HI! I AM GINNY was used by Vogue for the first time in 1951 to introduce their new wavette hair kits with the doll. This was a set of tiny plastic curlers in an acetate box kit that the doll carried. They were promoted as a pair of dolls; one with her hair still in the process of being curled and the other all combed out from the curling with hat on and ready to go. This was so succesful that buyers were sending in orders and re-ordering. Many, instead of designating the doll with the wavette hair kits, just wrote on order blanks to send GINNYS. Thus, the name caught on and this sparked the controversy over what the doll should be named. Mrs. Graves made the ultimate decision and named her for her own daughter, Virginia. 1951 also saw the continuation of some of their previous series with new additions such as KINDERGARTEN KIDDIES SERIES, BROTHER and SISTER SERIES, TINY MISS SERIES and FROLICKING FABLES SERIES which combined some of the former NURSERY RHYME, CHARACTER and FAR-AWAY PLACES SERIES.

As already pointed out, the early 1950's was a time of transition. From painted eye hard plastics to moving eye; mohair wigs to nutex and dynel wigs; and seemingly different finishes on the plastic. The earliest transitional moving eye plastic dolls seem to have a very delicate finish with pale coloring of lips and cheeks (these had mohair wigs). Others of the early 1950's had very fine finishes that somewhat resembled a porcelain doll. Some had a dull, bisque-like finish while others were somewhat shiny. No doubt that the much played-with dolls lost some of their original finish and, of course, the passing of time and exposure to all types of weather and humidity conditions had a lot to do with it. But, for some reason there seems to be more variation in the #3 Ginnys (non walkers) than in any of the other types. The introduction of PIXIE, named after Mrs. Graves' granddaughter, made 1952 a notable year. PIXIE had a poodle haircut in different shades of lambskin.

The Ginny CORONATION QUEEN was issued in 1953 in commemoration of the British Empire's Queen Elizabeth II's ascent to the throne. This doll was indeed a rare treasure to capture the heart of any little princess or grown-up collector for that matter. The doll's costume is a real tribute to its designer, Virginia Graves Carlson, for she had to dream up what the Queen would be attired in for her elaborate coronation ceremony and the gown was a top state secret. Coincidentally, it came quite close to the actual gown. It might be of interest here to relate some background information on the British coronations, especially since so many Americans have roots in Great Britain, not to mention our Canadian friends and the fact that many doll collectors are very much interested in the historical and cultural facts in connection with their doll collecting. The coronation of a British monarch is unrivalled in its grandeur, pomp and ceremony. St. Edward's crown, which our cover girl wears in miniature, is the official crown of England and is made of gold set with pearls and precious stones. The royal scepter is also gold and is the sovereign's emblem of authority. The coronation of a British queen is a remarkable event and the 25th anniversary is even more unusual. Only six women have ever been crowned queen of the British monarchy and only two celebrated their silver jubilee. Queen Elizabeth II has become the third longest reigning queen in Great Britain's history and she also is not only an extremely popular sovereign with her subjects but her popularity is worldwide because of her extensive travels. And so, at the time of publication of this book, Queen Elizabeth celebrates her Silver Jubilee, and it seems only fitting that we have chosen the CORONATION QUEEN GINNY to grace our cover.

By late 1953, six different outfits were offered with zippers, a very innovative thing at the time for the doll industry. Still a new range of outfits were added in groups like the following: DEBUTANTE SERIES, FABLE and BRIDE, GADABOUT SERIES, TWIN SERIES, KINDERGARTEN SCHOOL SERIES and KINDERGARTEN AFTERNOON SERIES. Ginny came with three hairstyles in different color dynel wigs, had a miniature suitcase, hat box with six hats and several fitted wardrobe chests. The first of her line of furniture also appeared, the E Z Do wardrobe which was made of heavy Kraft board in a wooden frame and was personalized GINNY.

GINNY WALKS in 1954; this is Ginny #4, marked GINNY on back along with VOGUE
DOLLS, INC. PAT. PENDING. MADE IN U. S. A. She still has the painted
eyelashes. The authentic line of GINNY furniture is introduced, all fine
wooden pieces made in Maine and painted Ginny pink. There was a youth bed,
boudoir chair, a trousseau tree and an attractively boxed Dream-Cozy set
consisting of her complete bedding. In addition there was Ginny's Pup,
#831, Ginny's Trip Mates and many new outfits in different groupings such
as: FOR RAIN OR SHINE, KINDER CROWD DRESSES, FOR FUN TIME, THE CANDY DANDY
SERIES, MY FIRST CORSAGE STYLES, THE WHIZ KIDS GROUP and several separate
coats and hats including white bunny fur.

Plastic eyelashes were added in 1955, making this Ginny #5 and the marking
on the back was the same as above except with the Pat. No. 2687594.

Baby sister, Ginnette arrived this year; she was soft vinyl plastic with painted
eyes and 8" high. A gym set is added to the line of furniture as well as a
pink wooden wardrobe with sliding doors, shelves inside and a place to hang
her clothes. There are many accessories such as ice and roller skates, golden
locket, beads, bracelet and bag sets, plastic hangers with her name on them,
hair curlers, eyeglasses, boxed shoes and socks and Ginny's own notepaper with
a picture of her with her pup, Sparkie. New groups of clothing are also added and include: MERRY MOPPETS, GINNY GYM KIDS, BRIDAL TROUSSEAU, BON BONS,
AND AWAY WE GO. There was a fitted bridal chest, an unfitted travel case
and several wardrobes with doll and clothes. Budget style outfits were
introduced this year and four styles of coats including pink and blue fur.

Ginny and Ginnette were appearing on television commercials this year and a
15 minute educational film starring Faye Emerson was shown all over the country
produced in cooperation with the editors of Parents' Magazine. It was a 16
mm sound film entitled, "The Dolls in Your Life".

In 1956 Ginny was given a doll house and dog house which was made of heavy
corrugated board. Her bedroom set was redesigned with the addition of a
rocking chair, table and chairs. There were many new accessories and outfits
added to the line and Ginnette was reissued with moving eyes. Ginny Doll Club began.

Big sister, Jill, appeared in 1957; she was a hard plastic doll with bending
knees and was 10 1/2 inches tall. Ginny was also redesigned with bending
knees and this makes her #6. Her marking was the same as #5. Ginny had 62
new outfits that year plus several more in three different fitted wardrobe
cases and trunks, a Party Package, Ginny's Apron set, a fitted trousseau chest,
a Knit Kit with instructions and yarn to make matching sweaters for Ginny,
Ginnette and Jill besides the line of furniture. (For both Ginny and Ginnette.)

1958 saw the introduction of baby brother Jimmy, same mold as the original
Ginnette; big brother Jeff, a 12"all vinyl doll with molded hair; and Jan, 10 1/2"
sister, vinyl doll with rooted hair. All Ginny Family Dolls are marked Vogue
on the back. There were over six dozen new outfits for Ginny, the accessory
and furniture line and eight Vogue patterns for Ginny and little girls.

Jimmy was discontinued in 1959. This year Ginny had some four dozen newly
designed outfits, a complete line of accessories and furniture. New Ginny's
FAR-AWAY LANDS boxed costumes were offered from seven countries: Israel,
Orient, Holland, Alaska, Hawaii, Scandinavia and the British Isles.

SOME INTERESTING GINNYS OF THE EARLY 1950's
Pictured at the right is a 1950 early hard
plastic Ginny with mohair wig and the very
pale facial coloring that shows up well in
this photo, even tho not in color. These
dolls are readily distinguishable from later
ones. They have a very appealing charm all
their own.

Below is a Ginny doll of 1953 that was
actually named GINGER by Vogue, thus pre-
dating the Ginger doll manufactured by
Cosmopolitan Doll Company at a later date.
Doll is courtesy of Bessie Carson and photo
and information is through the courtesy of
Pat and Dwight Smith: Pat Smith writes:
"This is a Vogue GINGER doll. Bessie
Carson has one in the original box. The
box is plain light pink and marked VOGUE
Dolls, Inc., FASHION LEADERS IN DOLL SOCIETY,
No. 64. (See actual picture of side of box
below.) Her original wrist tag on a dark blue
string is silver (look like foil bonded to
tag board). One side says GINGER No. 64
(printed) and the other side says A VOGUE
DOLL (script). Her original clothes are
a white organdy dress with multicolored
dots embroidered on, with attached white
taffeta slip, white taffeta bloomers and
white sox with red snap shoes. Red straw
hat trimmed with red satin ribbon with a
bunch of small rose petals. She is marked
VOGUE on her back and is elastic strung.
She is the same doll as the Ginny with
sleep eyes and painted lashes. Hairdo is
different as it is curled up in front so that
it frames her face. The dress is marked
VOGUE in script in blue on a white satin
ribbon tag."

60

Hi! — I am Ginny

(That's my twin sister — in curlers — sitting there)
We're the dolling pair known everywhere
cuz we've got such BEAUTIFLE HAIR
See— you can WET IT
Then COMB, CURL and SET IT
I'll stay just that way anywhere —
O — you never saw BEAUTIFLER HAIR!

* sez GINNY

* Honest! Our hair is so Beautifle (naturally curly "NUTEX") you just can't resist fixing it on our real plastic curlers — wetting it and setting it and then combing it out, just the way Mother gets hers done. And, like the rest of our Vogue Doll relations, we're Beautifle all over, from our cute little faces all down our chubby little selves. We're unbreakable cuz we're all plastic — and you can wash us and all our Exquisite clothes . . . so we stay Beautifle for ever 'n ever 'n ever.

Vogue Dolls, INC.
MEDFORD, MASS.

1951

Courtesy of Vogue

Ring The Bell...

OF YOUR CASH REGISTER!

THESE TWO SPECIAL CHRISTMAS DOLLS

MERRY LEE (on right) Red organdy dress — white trim with bells. Dashing red hair bow . . . . $24 PER DOZ.

HOLLY BELLE (on left) Red velvet bonnet with white feather. Dress with velvet yoke — Holly-trimmed white taffeta skirt. Bell on panties . . . . $27 PER DOZ.

ORDER NOW . . . be prepared for active Christmas holiday trade.

Vogue Dolls, INC.
MEDFORD, MASS.

KINDERGARTEN SERIES

So charming and pert in their fine little outfits! So exactly scaled to life and dressed to perfection! Each one will enchant a little girl . . . and the donor, too.

32 NAN . . . in taffeta and velvet

29 TINA . . . in chambray with floral trim

23 KAY . . . in dotted swiss and lace trim

$24.00 per dozen

POPULAR FAVORITES FOR YOUNG SPORTS

These authentic costumes will fill a great need in the doll world. Observant and bright children KNOW the difference and Vogue strives to cater to particular tastes.

SKI . . . pants, jacket with fur-like trim, ski set

ROLLER SKATER . . . plaid skating costume, skates

TENNIS . . . white dress, sweater, visor, racquet

$27.00 per dozen

ski

roller skater

tennis

SPORTS SERIES

LITTLE LADIES . . . BUT "OH, SO CUTE"!

TINY MISS SERIES

Can't you just imagine the thrill these crisp little ladies will give when they are received? Every child's dream is fulfilled by Vogue dolls.

41 JUNE . . . organdy dress with lace, straw hat

42 GLAD . . . ninon dress, ribbon bands, felt hat

43 BERL . . . flowered taffeta dress, felt hat

$27.00 per dozen

Courtesy of Vogue

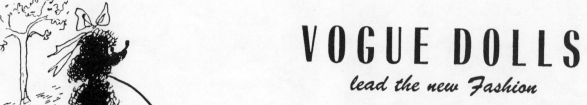

VOGUE DOLLS
lead the new Fashion

Yes . . . VOGUE DOLLS even beat LIFE MAGAZINE'S issue on Poodle Haircuts with their exciting, new poodle-cut wigs for 8" all-plastic dolls.

Poodle

*

POODLE haircuts are causing so much talk in the grown-up world of fashion that naturally the doll trade will need VOGUE DOLL's smart new poodle-cut, real lambskin wigs to satisfy the little girl's desire for fashionable dolls. These lifelike wigs are sure to sell more VOGUE DOLLS . . . so be sure your stock has PLENTY of them!

Vogue Dolls, INC.

* This is PIXIE, the granddaughter of our Founder, with her new Poodle Hairdo.

1952

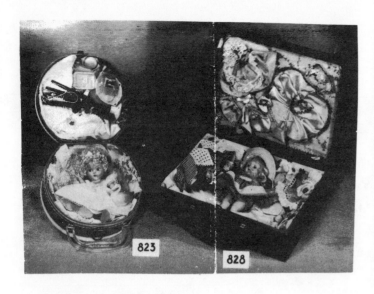

WE'RE BUSTIN' INSIDE
WITH JUSTIFIABLE PRIDE
OVER ALL THESE "CALLS"
WE GET FOR OUR DOLLS!

Just take a peek at these, please!

Vogue Dolls, INC.

Vogue photos

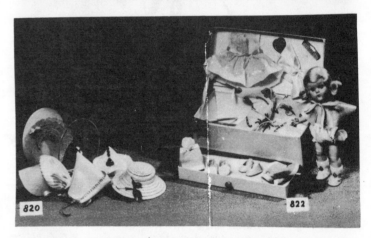

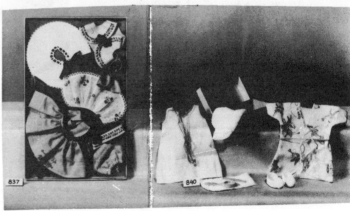

1952: Any little girl can dress and undress Vogue dolls and every little girl enjoys owning one or more of these adorable playthings. It is great fun to add extra sets of separate clothes and to make your doll's wardrobe as smart as your own! All clothes may be washed or dry cleaned and are easily changeable just like a real child's. Hat boxes, suitcases, chests and wardrobe trunks to hold the outfits and accessories are wonderful to have.

BROTHER & SISTER SERIES

TINY MISS SERIES

KINDERGARTEN SERIES

KINDERGARTEN SERIES

KINDERGARTEN SERIES

1952

DYNEL AND
LAMBSKIN WIGS
WITH POODLE HAIR DO
PIGTAILS OR CURLS

TINY MISS SERIES

DEBUTANTE SERIES

DEBUTANTE SERIES

JULIE WEE WILLIE ALICE SCOTCH
FROLICKING FABLES SERIES

INDIAN PRISCILLA JOHN ALDEN
FROLICKING FABLES SERIES

GINNY SERIES

80 81 86 85

SPORT SERIES

SKIER ICE SKATER ROLLER SKATER

FROLICKING FABLES SERIES

HOLLAND BOY HOLLAND GIRL

RODEO GIRL RODEO BOY

TYROLEAN TWINS: Boy and girl
of the European Alps in cunning
costumes of bright blue felt
with attached shadow organdy
tops. The boy wears bells
so that his family can hear
him up in the mountains when
he tends the flocks. These
outfits came in other colors. 1952

8'' FULLY JOINTED
ALL-PLASTIC DOLLS
WITH MOVING EYES
SHOES AND SOCKS

VOGUE DOLLS, INC.

FASHION LEADERS IN DOLL SOCIETY

33 SHIP AVENUE, MEDFORD 55, MASS. — MYstic 6-7030
DOLLS, SEPARATE CLOTHES, FITTED CASES AND ACCESSORIES

Terms — 2/10 Net 30 Days — F.O.B. Medford
No Anticipation

"See my new outfits with TALON ZIPPERS"

— DRESSED DOLLS —

NOTE: All dressed dolls individually packed in our *NEW* CARRY-ALL boxes

Style	Name	Description	Per Dozen
70	A. M.	Blue Denim Jeans; Red Check Skirt with ZIPPER Closing. Straw Hat; Eyeglasses; Snap Shoes and Socks; Braids.	$28.00
71	P. M.	Pink Batiste Nightie, Lace and Ribbon Trim. Aqua Percale Flower Print Robe with ZIPPER Closing, Ric-Rac Trim. Slippers; Candle and Candle-Holder; Braids.	31.50
72	School	Royal Blue Pencil Print Percale Dress and Panties, Yellow Bias Trim, ZIPPER Closing, Straw Hat with Daisy; Pocketbook; Snap Shoes and Socks; Braids.	31.50
73	Afternoon	Magenta Iridescent Silk Taffeta Dress and Panties, Lace and Black Velvet Ribbon Trim and ZIPPER Closing. Petticoat with Cascading Net Ruffles. Straw Hat with Flowers. Snap Shoes and Socks. Regular Side Part Hair-do.	34.50
74	Party	White All-Nylon Dress with Nylon Lace Ruffles, Flowers and Ribbon Bow Trim, Ribbon Sash and ZIPPER Closing; Pink Taffeta Petticoat and Panties; Straw Hat, Flower Trim; Snap Shoes and Socks; Bang Hair-do.	42.00
75	Stormy Weather	Yellow Plastic Slicker Coat with SEPARATING ZIPPER Closing. So'-wester Hat; Black Boots and Socks. Complete outfit under Slicker. Separate Bag Containing Snap Shoes and Hat. Eyeglasses; Braids.	42.00

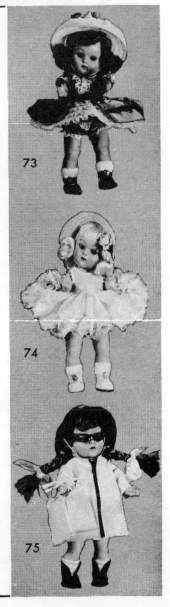

1953

hi! I'm Ginny

The Fashion Leader in Doll Society
Look At All My Lovely Outfits

It's fun to change Ginny's hair-do to match your own

Her hair can be dampened, put up in curlers . . .

and set in a variety of different hairstyles as illustrated

Ginny, the Vogue Doll is a masterpiece in miniature. She is 8 inches tall, made of unbreakable plastic, with moving arms and legs. Open-shut eyes in brown or blue. Available in three hairstyles — Ginny bangs, pigtails or side part.

Everyone has fun dressing and undressing little Ginny. She has more than 50 different outfits that you can buy separately to enlarge her wardrobe. And all of the dainty garments can be easily washed or dry cleaned. Hat boxes, suitcases, wardrobe trunks and the miniature E-Z-DO wardrobe closet are perfect for storing Ginny's outfits and accessories.

Have fun . . . start your Vogue Doll Collection

FASHION LEADERS IN DOLL SOCIETY

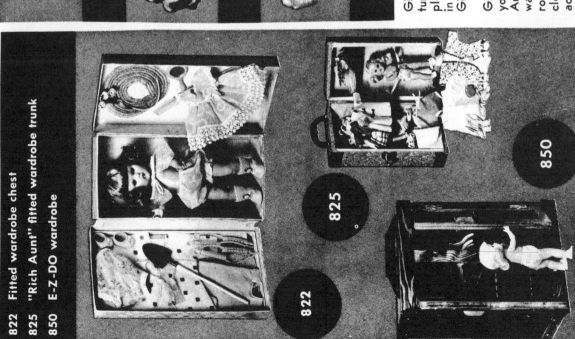

822 Fitted wardrobe chest
825 "Rich Aunt" fitted wardrobe trunk
850 E-Z-DO wardrobe

822

825

850

Linda
21

Donna
22

Pat
31

Nan
32

Kay
23

April
24

Tina
29

Dawn
30

Connie
25

Carol
26

Hope
27

Margie
28

KINDERGARTEN AFTERNOON
SERIES

1953

KINDERGARTEN SCHOOL
SERIES

71

Dutch Boy 35

Dutch Girl 36

June 41

Glad 42

Hansel 33

Beryl 43

Gretel 34

Cheryl 44

Cowboy 37

Lucy 39

Cowgirl 38

Wanda 40

• TWIN SERIES • • TINY MISS SERIES •

1953

72

Toddles or composition Ginnys:
Left above and clockwise.

Alice in Wonderland, 1943, from Character
and Nursery Rhyme Dolls. All cotton outfit has separate panties and attached
petticoat. A blue cotton twill label
is sewn in back at the waist.

Oriental from an early Far-Away Lands
series about 1944. Cotton print kimona
is worn over jumpsuit that closes in
back with a tie string. The kimona would
seem to indicate that the doll represents
Japan but CHINESE GIRL is stamped on the
bottom of right shoe. Courtesy of Sonny
Hemmi.

Little girl in pink organdy has no label
in dress, but the hook and eye closing
used in the back of the outfit would
date it in the late forties. Panties
are fashioned in one piece with the
dress.

Gypsy girl is an R & B marked
doll, dressed by Vogue. Date
is early 1940's. Organdy
panties are attached to blouse
and rayon skirt has elastic
waist. Blouse closes in the
back with a string tie.

Two below are from the 1943
Character and Nursery Rhyme
Dolls:

Wee Willie Winkie's pajamas
are cotton flannel. Note
blue cotton twill label.

Mistress Mary's outfit is
cotton and worn over long
pantalets.

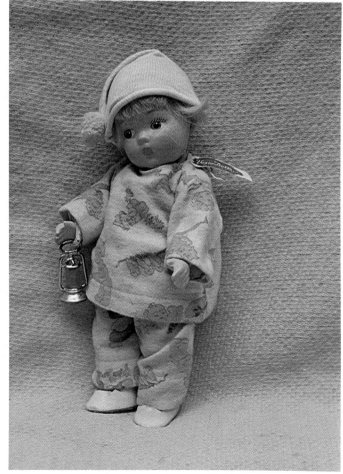

This is a study in Baby Ginny Dolls. Above left is the composition SUNSHINE BABY of 1943, the baby version of TODDLES. Doll is the same construction as Toddles except for the baby curved legs. Dress is organdy with separate panties and slip. Courtesy of Marge Meisinger. Above right is the hard plastic baby from the CRIB CROWD series of 1950. This doll is unusual in that the eyes are painted looking to the left. Out-fit is printed organdy and closes in the back with hook and eye; there is no tag. These dolls wore special ringlet wigs, a rather wiry poodle cut fashion sewn on to the base in rows.

CRIB CROWD baby, RUTHIE #836, 1950. Eyes look to the right which is typical of most of this series. Garment is printed organdy over a cotton attached slip and rubber panties. There is a tie string closing in back of dress which also has the blue and white VOGUE tag. Doll won a blue ribbon in a Doll Show modern catefory in Florida, 1976.

TINY MISS SERIES

*TINY MISS Series, 1951.
#39 LUCY; striped cotton and organdy.*

#40 WANDA; dimity with ribbon trim.

#41 JUNE; organdy with baby rick rack trim.

All dolls wear real straw bonnets.

#42 GLAD; cotton with braid trim.

#43 BERL; gingham check with ribbons.

#44 CHERYL; taffeta with net trim.

All dolls have matching panties and wear middle snap leatherette shoes.

TINY MISS SERIES

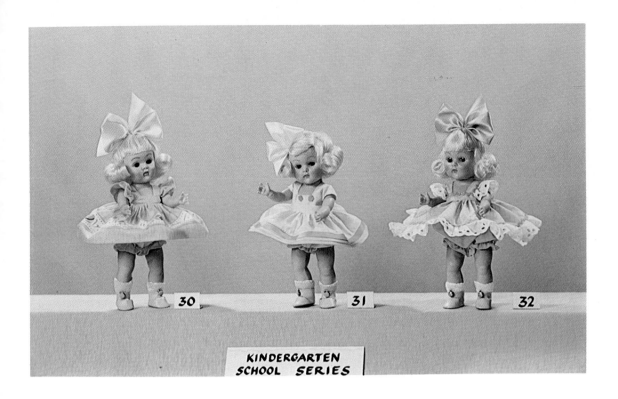

KINDERGARTEN SCHOOL SERIES

KINDERGARTEN SCHOOL SERIES: #30 DAWN; cotton chambray pinafore. #31 PAT; cotton pique with bias trim. #32 NAN; embossed cotton with eyelet ruffles. All dolls in this series had big hair ribbons, matching panties and leatherette shoes. Others in the series were named: LINDA, DONNA, KAY, APRIL, CONNIE, CAROL, HOPE, MARGIE and TINA. This was the same year that the name GINNY was first introduced. 1951.

All photographs on thes pages by Eric Muller for Vogue.

TRAVEL TRUNKS show variety of clothes and accessories available in 1951.

TWIN SERIES, 1953; COWBOY and COWGIRL. Costumes were fashioned of wool felt with attached cotton tops. The girl's outfit had attached felt panties.

DUTCH COUPLE. Clothes are made of cotton with the girl's hat and apron of printed organdy with eyelet embroidery trim. The boy sports a wool felt scarf.

Photos by Eric Muller for Vogue

GINNY was an ACTION DOLL and so she's all set for anything. Above left and clockwise: Horseback riding with felt jodhpurs, boots and riding hat; skiing in a gaily
embroidered jacket and hat with wool mittens; at the beach with cotton terry lined
jacket and hat and striped beach towel; and ready for the rainstorm in a rainset
with umbrella that matches her outfit.

Upper left and clockwise: Taffeta plaid formal with velvet bodice and hat.
CINDERELLA and PRINCE CHARMING; her outfit is printed organdy with velvet
paniers and the Prince's uniform is wool felt. Below are two SOUTHERN BELLES,
one in polished cotton stripes and the other in cotton batiste. Cinderella
courtesy of Marge Meisinger.

Angela
65

Ginger
64

Alice
51

Red Riding Hood
52

Cathy
61

Pamela
60

Bo-Peep
53

Mistress Mary
54

Karen
63

Becky
62

Bride
55

Brides-maid
56

• DEBUTANTE SERIES •   • FABLE AND BRIDE SERIES •

1953

81

840 Miniature suitcase
820 Acetate hat box with six hats in each box

828 "Rich Uncle" fitted red suitcase — wooden foundation 9" x 12"

840
828
Ballet 45
820
T.V. 46

• GADABOUT SERIES •

Ski 49
Ice Skater 50
Roller Skater 47
Beach 48

• GADABOUT SERIES •   • GADABOUT SERIES •

Last sheet of 1953 booklet

TRUE STORIES about GINNY (From October 1957 GINNY DOLL NEWS)

A very little girl was noticed in a large New England Food Store busily moving articles on the shelves, piling some of them on the floor. From around the corner, her mother appeared and said, "Why, Ann, for goodness sakes, what are you doing?" The little girl looked up in disgust and said, "I'm looking for the Ginny dolls. Don't they sell them in this store?"

While visiting in a home in Pasadena this past summer, an 11 year old girl was asked if she had a Ginny doll. The little girl was amazed that she should be asked such a question. Her reply was, "Of course, I have lots of Ginny dolls. Everyone in my class has Ginny dolls. You would not be in the 'swim', if you did not own one."

SOME INTERESTING GINNYS OF THE 1950's.
Vogue introduced a hard plastic black
Ginny in 1953: these were referred to as
Negro Ginnys. This is the painted
lashed, non walker, wearing a pink
tutu with taffeta top. This also
seems to be the first record of Vogue
using brown eyes on their sleep eye
Ginnys which they continued over the
years altho they seem to be more rare
than blue eyed dolls.

The same head was also used on a walker
body. Jo Ann Zipperer has this doll in
its original box and mint outfit of
yellow embossed cotton with white top,
green felt hat and green accessories.
Clothing tag is rayon and she also
has wrist tag. The date of this is
1954, of course, the date that Ginny
first became a walker. Incidentally,
the inventor of the walking mechanism
for Ginny was Mr. Henry Paul Cleaver
and the mechanism was patented as
#2,687,594, dated August 31, 1954,
but actually filed on June 12, 1953.
The U. S. Patent Office contains the
five page descriptive report detailing
the invention of a walking and sitting
doll.

Ginny as DAVY CROCKETT was a special
outfit of 1955 to promote summer sales.
Simulated suede was used to resemble buck
skin for the jacket and pants with fringe,
belt and Kentucky-type rifle. There was
also an authentic fur cap, a Davy Crockett emblem and button.

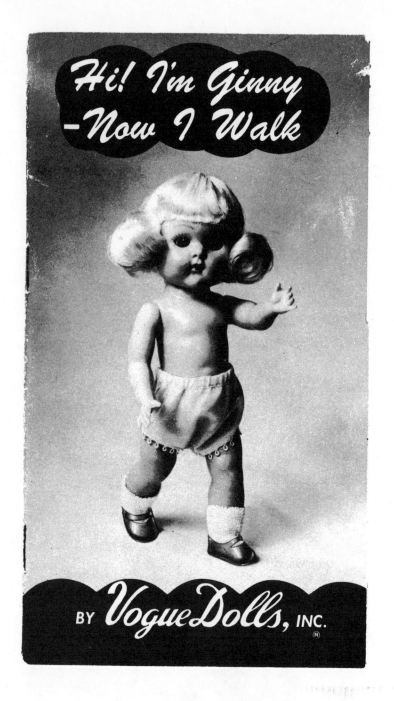

Here's how I walk

It's easy to make me walk just like any little girl walks, if you follow these simple instructions. Just be sure my legs are straight, as yours are when you are standing still.

Put your thumb and fingers under my arms from the back and walk me on any ordinary surface. If the surface is too slippery, like glass for example, my feet will slide just as yours do on ice. Besides walking, I also sit, stand and sleep.

1954 BOOKLET; MORE SHEETS ON FOLLOWING PAGES

TRUE STORIES about GINNY (Reprinted from November, 1957 GINNY DOLL NEWS)

A lady was on her way to work one morning with her little niece whom she was leaving at her school. Her niece had Ginny with her. A friend came by and offered them a ride. The little girl refused to get into the car. So, they walked to school. The aunt could not understand why the child would not accent the ride. In questioning her, the little girl replied, "My mother told me not to accept a ride from anyone I did not know and I have told Ginny the same thing. Ginny did not know the lady who offered the ride."

A woman in a department store was purchasing a Ginny doll and remarked to the saleslady, "I have a little boy at home with a bad case of measles. He said if he only had TWO Ginny dolls he would get better quickly."

No. 181
COTTON COAT

My brown checked coat and straw bonnet for Spring-like days makes me feel very smart.

No. 282
FELT COAT

For colder days you will love my rose or blue colored felt coat with matching fur trimmed hat.

No. 51 Dressed Doll   No. 52 Dressed Doll   No. 53 Dressed Doll
No. 351 Outfit Only   No. 352 Outfit Only   No. 353 Outfit Only

THE CANDY DANDY SERIES

No. 383
VELVET COAT

For very special occasions I like to wear my fur trimmed red or green velvet princess coat, hat and muff of white fur.

No. 484
FUR COAT

I'll be nice and warm in my white bunny coat, hat and muff.

No. 54 Dressed Doll   No. 55 Dressed Doll   No. 56 Dressed Doll
No. 354 Outfit Only   No. 355 Outfit Only   No. 356 Outfit Only

My Accessories are very special, too!

Now that you have seen my beautiful outfits you'll want to see my very special accessories, too. All of them are made just for me and I think they are exciting. There are Wardrobes to help you hang my clothes neatly just like grown-ups do. For traveling I have a Train Case, a Fitted Wardrobe Trunk and a Fitted Weekender Suitcase. These three pieces of luggage are adorable in a matched color combination. You'll see many other accessories in this book even to my little Puppy. There isn't even room to show them all here! Besides the ones you see in the pictures, I have a set of four Separate Curlers and a Cosmetic Cape with instructions for curling my hair, and I also have Ice Shoe Skates, Roller Shoe Skates and even a Poodle Wig with directions for using it. I think you'll find my accessories exciting, too!

No. 33 Dressed Doll   No. 35 Dressed Doll   No. 37 Dressed Doll
No. 233 Outfit Only   No. 234 Outfit Only   No. 235 Outfit Only

MY TWIN SETS

No. 34 Dressed Doll   No. 36 Dressed Doll   No. 38 Dressed Doll
No. 236 Outfit Only   No. 237 Outfit Only   No. 238 Outfit Only

No. 822
FITTED WARDROBE CHEST

My Fitted Wardrobe Chest holds me with shoes, socks, dress and straw hat, panties, plastic cosmetic cape, playsuit, bathrobe, nightie, slippers, comb, mirror, towel, curlers and toy.

No. 851
GINNY'S EYEGLASSES

I feel real grown up when I put on my glasses. I have red, blue and amber ones to go with my everyday outfits. I save my gold ones for extra special occasions.

No. 842
SHOE BAG AND SHOES

My gay plaid Shoe Bag holds two extra pairs of shoes. It can be attached to my E-Z-Do Wardrobe door with thumb tacks.

A Message from the Maker of Ginny

Ginny is the most popular doll of her size in the world today. Each year we receive thousands of letters from little girls, and from their mothers too, telling us how much they enjoy playing with Ginny. This is really not surprising when you consider that Ginny was created by a world famous sculptor. She is made of unbreakable plastic to last for years. Ginny's clothes are designed by my daughter, Virginia Graves, and competent critics have been kind enough to call them the finest dolls' clothes made. Ginny's dainty clothes are custom made by experienced dressmakers and have hooks and eyes — some have zippers — to make it easy for little fingers to dress and undress her easily. The clothes are noted for accurate fit and are sturdily made for long wear. Ginny has more accessories and in a wider variety than any other doll. We know you'll love her just as much as we do.

Jennie H. Graves
President

Vogue Dolls, Inc.

33 SHIP AVENUE, MEDFORD 55, MASSACHUSETTS

Ptd. in U.S.A.

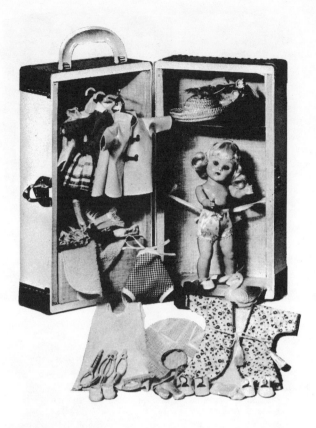

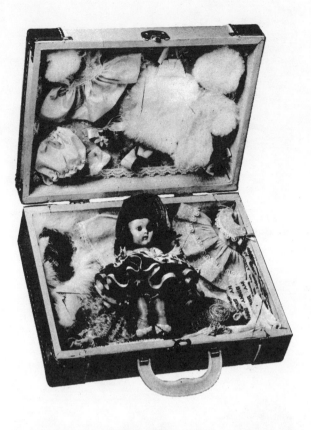

No. 826   FITTED WARDROBE TRUNK
My Wardrobe, which matches my Train Case and Weekender luggage, holds me, rain slicker and sou'wester, boots, three dresses and panties, two straw hats, plastic cosmetic cape, curlers, playsuit, bathrobe, nightie, slippers, one pair extra shoes and socks and toy.

No. 829   FITTED WEEKENDER
Here I am in my Weekender Suitcase which matches my Train Case and Wardrobe. I'm all dressed up and ready to go with my ice skater outfit and skates; silk dress and panties; organdy dress, panties and straw hat; white bunny fur coat, hat and muff; jersey Ginny sweater set; pocketbook, corsage, extra shoes and socks, nightie and zipper robe, slippers and towel.

No. 45   Dressed Doll   No. 46   Dressed Doll   No. 47   Dressed Doll
No. 345 Outfit Only   No. 346 Outfit Only   No. 347 Outfit Only

FOR FUN TIME

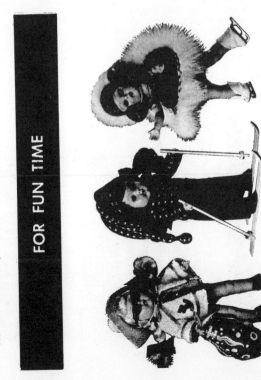

No. 48   Dressed Doll   No. 49   Dressed Doll   No. 50   Dressed Doll
No. 348 Outfit Only   No. 349 Outfit Only   No. 350 Outfit Only

No. 831
GINNY'S PUP

I have lots of fun walking with my wire haired terrier. He is so proud of his little plaid blanket that he gets frisky and I have to hold him by his leash.

No. 27 Dressed Doll   No. 28 Dressed Doll   No. 29 Dressed Doll
No. 127 Outfit Only   No. 128 Outfit Only   No. 129 Outfit Only

No. 840
MINIATURE SUITCASE

My Miniature Suitcase is just crowded with a bathrobe, nightie, slippers, towel, comb and mirror.

FOR RAIN OR SHINE

No. 820
HAT BOX

My peek-a-boo Hat Box has five hats to give variety to my wardrobe.

No. 30 Dressed Doll   No. 31 Dressed Doll   No. 32 Dressed Doll
No. 130 Outfit Only   No. 131 Outfit Only   No. 132 Outfit Only

I'm the "Fashion Leader in Doll Society"®

I have been known as "The Fashion Leader in Doll Society" by little girls and their mothers everywhere. I am eight inches tall and made of unbreakable plastic. You can have me with either brown or blue eyes and my hair comes in lovely shades of blonde, brunette and auburn. You can buy me with either bangs or pigtails and you can dampen and set my life-like Dynel hair in many different hair styles.

You will have loads of fun dressing and undressing me. I have more than fifty different outfits which you can buy separately. As you look through this book you will see me modeling these beautiful outfits, which are custom made by skilled dressmakers. Each outfit has its own tiny "Vogue Doll, Inc." label inside it. Many of my trimmings, flowers and hats are imported from fashion centers in Europe. I have outfits for every occasion. Every minute in the day I'm the best dressed little doll in the world! Just see my sun, rain and snow outfits, play clothes, school dresses, dainty nylon lace party dress and some of my styles even have real zippers just like grown up clothes.

You'll love my many wonderful accessories. They were made just for me and will give you lots of fun when you play with me at home or when you take me on a trip.

88

No. 39 Dressed Doll   No. 40 Dressed Doll   No. 41 Dressed Doll
No. 239 Outfit Only   No. 240 Outfit Only   No. 241 Outfit Only

MY TINY MISS STYLES

No. 42 Dressed Doll   No. 43 Dressed Doll   No. 44 Dressed Doll
No. 242 Outfit Only   No. 243 Outfit Only   No. 244 Outfit Only

No. 850
E-Z-DO WARDROBE

Here I am peeking into my miniature E-Z-Do Wardrobe which comes equipped with hangers for my clothes and shelves to hold my hats and tiny accessories. It is sturdily made, just like Mommy's big E-Z-Do Wardrobe, with swinging doors that fasten easily.

No. 21 Dressed Doll
No. 121 Outfit Only

No. 22 Dressed Doll
No. 122 Outfit Only

No. 23 Dressed Doll
No. 123 Outfit Only

MY KINDER CROWD DRESSES

No. 24 Dressed Doll
No. 124 Outfit Only

No. 25 Dressed Doll
No. 125 Outfit Only

No. 26 Dressed Doll
No. 126 Outfit Only

| No. 60 Dressed Doll | No. 61 Dressed Doll | No. 62 Dressed Doll | | No. 70 Dressed Doll | No. 71 Dressed Doll | No. 72 Dressed Doll |
| No. 460 Outfit Only | No. 461 Outfit Only | No. 462 Outfit Only | | No. 670 Outfit Only | No. 671 Outfit Only | No. 672 Outfit Only |

MY FIRST CORSAGE STYLES   THE WHIZ KIDS GROUP

| No. 63 Dressed Doll | No. 64 Dressed Doll | No. 65 Dressed Doll | | No. 73 Dressed Doll | No. 74 Dressed Doll | No. 75 Dressed Doll |
| No. 463 Outfit Only | No. 464 Outfit Only | No. 465 Outfit Only | | No. 673 Outfit Only | No. 674 Outfit Only | No. 675 Outfit Only |

No. 830
GINNY'S TRIP MATES
I am very excited about my new Trip Mates. I have a garment bag with hangers, a car bag for traveling, a swag bag, and a hat bag. They are all in attractive gay matching plaid and have real zippers.

No. 823 UNFITTED TRAIN CASE
My smart sturdy train case can hold me and plenty of clothes. It comes empty and matches my Fitted Wardrobe and Weekender luggage.

Hi! ... I'm Ginny

see all my beautiful clothes →

CREATIONS OF
VOGUE DOLLS inc.

what shall I wear today?

1955

KINDER CROWD

No. 21 Dressed Doll	No. 22 Dressed Doll	No. 23 Dressed Doll	No. 24 Dressed Doll	No. 25 Dressed Doll	No. 26 Dressed Doll
No. 121 Outfit Only	No. 122 Outfit Only	No. 123 Outfit Only	No. 124 Outfit Only	No. 125 Outfit Only	No. 126 Outfit Only

GINNY GYM KIDS

No. 27 Dressed Doll	No. 28 Dressed Doll	No. 29 Dressed Doll	No. 30 Dressed Doll	No. 31 Dressed Doll	No. 32 Dressed Doll
No. 127 Outfit Only	No. 128 Outfit Only	No. 129 Outfit Only	No. 130 Outfit Only	No. 131 Outfit Only	No. 132 Outfit Only

AND AWAY WE GO

| No. 51 Dressed Doll | No. 52 Dressed Doll | No. 53 Dressed Doll | No. 54 Dressed Doll | No. 55 Dressed Doll | No. 56 Dressed Doll |
| No. 351 Outfit Only | No. 352 Outfit Only | No. 353 Outfit Only | No. 354 Outfit Only | No. 355 Outfit Only | No. 356 Outfit Only |

BON-BONS

| No. 80 Dressed Doll | No. 81 Dressed Doll | No. 82 Dressed Doll | No. 83 Dressed Doll | No. 84 Dressed Doll | No. 85 Dressed Doll |
| No. 580 Outfit Only | No. 581 Outfit Only | No. 582 Outfit Only | No. 583 Outfit Only | No. 584 Outfit Only | No. 585 Outfit Only |

1955

TRUE STORY about GINNY (Reprinted from November 1957 GINNY CLUB NEWS)

One of the ladies in the Vogue office received a letter from her friend who had twin girls. They had just moved into a lovely new home. There was a beautiful electric stove with a glass oven door in the kitchen. The little twins were gazing through the door of the oven with their Ginny dolls. The mother asked them to go away from the stove. "Oh, dear," said one of the girls, "Ginny likes to see the cookies breathing!"

MERRY MOPPETS

No. 33 Dressed Doll	No. 34 Dressed Doll	No. 35 Dressed Doll	No. 36 Dressed Doll	No. 37 Dressed Doll	No. 38 Dressed Doll
No. 233 Outfit Only	No. 234 Outfit Only	No. 235 Outfit Only	No. 236 Outfit Only	No. 237 Outfit Only	No. 238 Outfit Only

TINY MISS

No. 39 Dressed Doll	No. 40 Dressed Doll	No. 41 Dressed Doll	No. 42 Dressed Doll	No. 43 Dressed Doll	No. 44 Dressed Doll
No. 239 Outfit Only	No. 240 Outfit Only	No. 241 Outfit Only	No. 242 Outfit Only	No. 243 Outfit Only	No. 244 Outfit Only

1955

TRUE STORY about GINNY (Reprinted from November 1957 GINNY CLUB NEWS)

Mrs. Graves was recently at the airport in Detroit when she noticed a sweet little
girl with a big bag. She went up to her and asked her if she had a Ginny doll.
In disgust, the small girl said, Of course, and they are all with me." She put her
hand in the bag and produced four Ginnys.

FUN TIME

No.45 Dressed Doll	No.46 Dressed Doll	No.47 Dressed Doll	No.48 Dressed Doll	No.49 Dressed Doll	No.50 Dressed Doll
No.345 Outfit Only	No.346 Outfit Only	No.347 Outfit Only	No.348 Outfit Only	No.349 Outfit Only	No.350 Outfit Only

BRIDAL TROUSSEAU

No.60 Dressed Doll	No.61 Dressed Doll	No.62 Dressed Doll	No.63 Dressed Doll	No.64 Dressed Doll	No.65 Dressed Doll
No.460 Outfit Only	No.461 Outfit Only	No.462 Outfit Only	No.463 Outfit Only	No.464 Outfit Only	No.465 Outfit Only

1955

Ginny's back to school again
Busy, and happy as can be
She's wearing her cute dresses
And leads in doll society.

GINNY CLUB NEWS 1956

94

No. 180 — My Navy Blue Coat with white collar and cuffs and my Straw Hat is my Sunday best coat.

No. 181 — This Black and White Check Coat, trimmed with red, with my red Beret for school days.

No. 182 — For rainy days my Yellow Zippered Rain Slicker, Sou'wester Hat and Boots.

No. 183 — I dress up in my Velvet Coat, pompon trim with a Fur Beret and Muff in either red or aqua.

No. 184 — For very special occasions, my Bunny Fur Coat and Hat comes in pink, blue, or white Fur.

    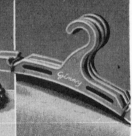

No. 845 — My Curlers and Cosmetic Cape are for setting my hair.

No. 847 — Look at a pair of Ice Skates and Socks just for me.

No. 848 — There is a pair of my own Roller Skates.

No. 835 — My Golden Locket is engraved with my name.

No. 836 — This new "B B B" set has a string of Beads, a matching Bracelet

No. 844 — My own set of six Hangers, with my name, for my clothes.

No. 866 — My Fitted Bridal Chest is a dream. It is made of hardwood, in pink and white, with swing-away trays, lined with silk lace ruffles and ribbon bows. I am dressed in my Bride Outfit, and in addition you will find my Fur Coat and Hat, complete Party Dress Outfit, complete Bon Bon Oufit, Jersey Swearer Outfit, Complete Going-Away Suit, Nylon Nightie and Peignoir, Rain Cape and Umbrella, Golden Locket, extra Shoes and Socks, Gold Eyeglasses, Corsage, Curlers, Comb and Mirror.

No. 925 — Here's my very own Gym Set with a real Swing, Slide, and Glider, that really works just like a big outdoor gym. The frame is of sturdy hardwood, the Swing is hung on real chains, and the Slide has a stainless steel surface. You'll have lots of fun playing with me on this Gym.

Vogue photos

No. 185 — My two piece Cotton Pajamas have lace and ribbon bow trim in assorted colors.

No. 186 — My Flowered Robe with zipper, collar, and net ruffle trim comes in different colors.

No. 187 — Protect my dresses on rainy days with my Plastic Hooded Raincape with my name in gold.

No. 188 — My Budget Style Dresses and Outfits come in many styles and colors.

No. 860 — My pink and white monogrammed Case includes Me in silk Panties, Shoes and Socks; with a Taffeta and Velvet Party Dress, and a Cotton School Dress with Plastic Belt and Straw Hat, on Hangers, extra Shoes and Socks.

No. 862 — This pink and white, metal covered Fitted Wardrobe Trunk, monogrammed with my name and picture, includes Me dressed in a Taffeta Party Dress, Panties, Shoes and Socks, and a Straw Hat. It also contains a Hooded Plastic Rain Cape, Flannel Pajamas, Sport Dress with Sweater, on Hangers. The Drawer holds my Nightie, Curlers, extra Panties, Cap, Tennis Racket, Rake, Slippers with Pompons, and extra Shoes.

No. 864 — My pink and white, metal covered Unfitted Travel Case is big enough to hold Me and lots and lots of my clothes, when you go on a trip, and it matches my other travel cases.

No. 865 — My pink and white, metal covered Holiday Fitted Wardrobe Trunk, with drawer, contains Me in my Ice Skating Outfit, and on Hangers you will find my Zippered House Coat, two piece lace-trimmed Pajamas, Taffeta Party Dress with Panties, Ski Outfit including Skis and Poles, Fur Coat and Beret, Slippers with Pompons, extra Shoes and Socks.

No. 864

TO GINNY'S LITTLE MOTHERS

I know that you'll enjoy playing with Ginny. Each year we receive thousands of letters from little girls and their mothers telling us how much fun they have with Ginny. She is made of unbreakable plastic, she has eyelashes, she walks, sits, stands, sleeps, and you can set her dynel hair in many styles. She's beautiful and you'll love her for years to come.

MY OWN ACCESSORIES

I have my very own accessories, cases, and furniture for added fun when you play with me at home, or when you take me on a trip. They are all very special, and many of them are monogrammed with my name and even my dainty pink and white matching furniture is made just to fit me. You will spend many happy days with me and my accessories.

CREATIONS OF   1955
VOGUE DOLLS inc.
33 SHIP AVENUE, MEDFORD 55, MASS.

No. 831 — I go walk-
ing with my Puppy
with his own little
Plaid Blanket and
Leash.

No. 840 — My Minia-
ture Suitcase has a
Bathrobe, Nightie,
Slippers, Towel, Comb
and Mirror.

No. 833 — Made just
for me are these Color-
ful Parasols that really
work like a big Um-
brella.

No. 852 — Now you
can have a new Wig
for me, either Bang
Roll or Braid, in
Blonde, Brunette, or
Auburn.

No. 821 — Choose
separate, trimmed Felt
or Straw Hats to match
my different dresses.

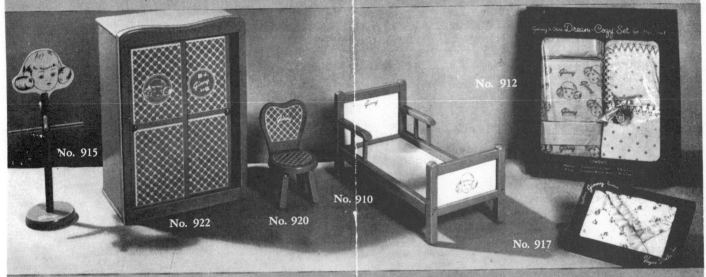

No. 915

No. 922

No. 920

No. 910

No. 912

No. 917

No. 910 — Here's my dainty Bed, made of hardwood, finished
in pink and white enamel, monogrammed with my name and
picture.

No. 912 — My Dream Cozy Bed Set has a plastic-covered,
fibre glass filled heat-sealed Mattress and Pillow, contoured
colored Bottom Sheet, contoured colored Top Sheet, printed
all over with my name and picture, Pillow Case and colored
Spread.

No. 915 — I hang my clothes on my matching personalized
Trousseau Tree.

No. 917 — My Rayon Quilted Puff keeps me warm and cozy.

No. 920 — My Chair, with my name is just the right size for
Me and is sturdily made of hardwood, in pink and white.

No. 922 — My new Wardrobe, in pink and white, with my
monogram, has a sturdy wood frame, sliding doors, shelves
for my Hats and Shoes, and Hangers for my Dresses.

No. 872 — I have
my own Note
Paper, printed in
five colors with a
Ginny Pencil in
each box.

No. 843 — My
Shoe Box holds
one pair of Shoes
and Socks, and
they come in as-
sorted colors.

No. 851 — Four
pair of my Eye-
glasses are in as-
sorted colors.

No. 870 — These
Metal Stands help
me to stand safely.

1955

97

The GINNY DOLL CLUB for small girls began in 1956. Pictured above, left, are the membership pins given to each member who also received a portrait of Ginny, shown upper right. On the following pages is a copy of the membership certificate and a reprint of the club's paper, GINNY CLUB NEWS, volume I, number 1. This was issued quarterly and was distributed to around 6,000 girls. The club continued until 1960. Membership kit was donated to the Ginny Doll Club for doll collectors in 1973 by Marge Meisinger who wrote, "this is my gift to the club for bringing Ginny anew to so many people who must be delighted as I am".

1956 Christmas Card sent by Vogue to their employees. It read inside, "A Merry, Merry Christmas and a Very Happy New Year" and was signed, "Ginny and Ginnette". For the 1955 card see it in color on the inside back cover. Cards designed by artist, Marion Quimby. Courtesy of Jennie Davis

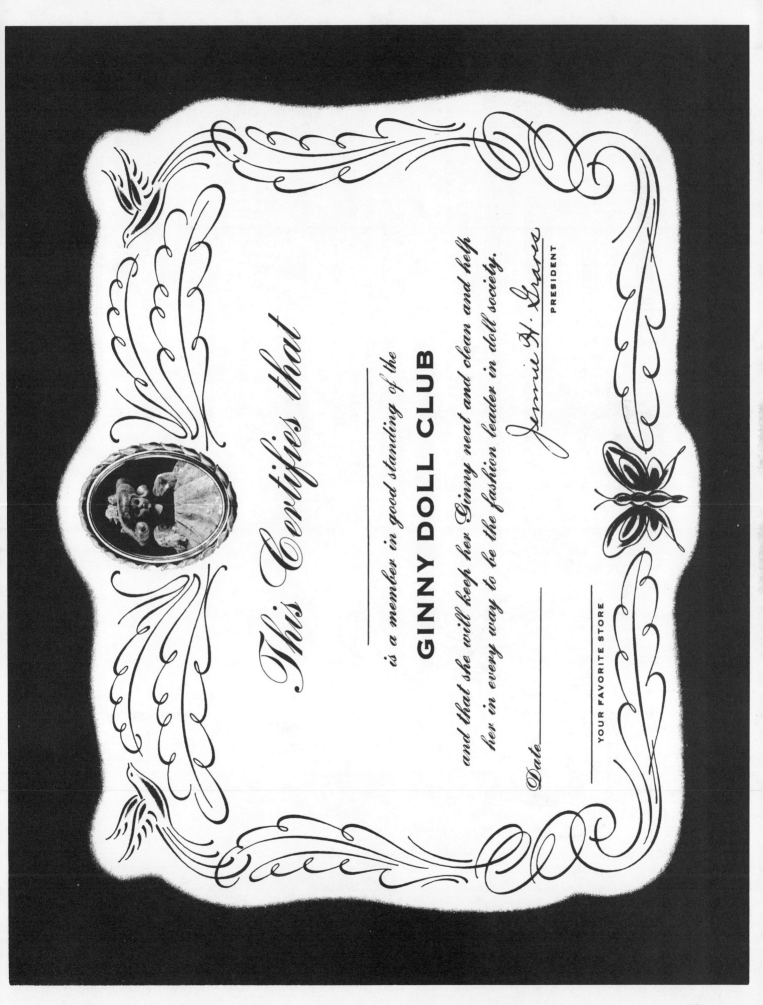

This Certifies that

_____

is a member in good standing of the

GINNY DOLL CLUB

and that she will keep her Ginny neat and clean and help
her in every way to be the fashion leader in doll society.

Jennie H. Graves

PRESIDENT

Date _____

_____

YOUR FAVORITE STORE

Ginny Club News

...and news of Ginnette, too.

VOGUE DOLLS, INC.   Fashion Leaders in Doll Society

TO LITTLE GIRLS EVERYWHERE

We are bubbling over with excitement, and know that you will be too. This is our first issue of the Ginny Club News, which will appear every few months. Now, we can all work and play together.

Ginny Clubs are springing up all over the country. We just had to tell Ginny and Ginnette about it, and were they pleased! The "little mothers" of Ginny are the members, and also Ginny herself. These Clubs are lots of fun. Do you have a Ginny Club in your neighborhood? If not, why don't you start one? This is how it could be done --

Ask all the little girls who own Ginnies to meet at someone's house, and tell them about your plan. Your Mother, we know, will help you with suggestions.

Choose a day and a definite time.
Meet at the different homes, and, of course, be sure that Ginny is there.
Let's have Jennie H. Graves as your Honorary National President.
Then, you will want your own Club Officers, - President, Secretary, Treasurer, and maybe even Committees.
Each girl could tell what her Ginny has been doing.
Social, games, etc.
Refreshments (Mother's help again)

Do you like to color? Try this:

New Fashions

Ginny has so many new outfits, – more than sixty, – lucky Ginny.

Navy coat, white collar and cuffs.

Yellow polished cotton dress, with velvet trimmings.

Pink and gray organdy, ribbon sash.

WHAT'S THE DIFFERENCE?

Four little pictures. They all look alike, don't they? BUT, one is different. See how quickly you can spot it.

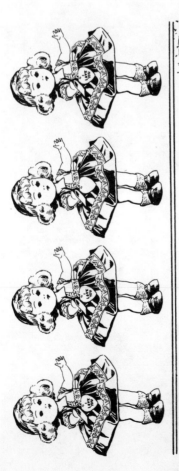

STORK CLUB PARTY

Do you know that we had a Cake and Coke Party at the Stork Club in New York, in March? Jennie H. Graves was the hostess. 114 children were there, including young patients from hospitals. Among the celebrities was Jayne Mansfield, and her lovely little daughter, and many other well-known actresses.

Ginny and Ginnette entertained, and gave a "sneak" preview of their adorable new styles. They also had the leads in the movie which was shown, "Dolls in Your Life", starring Faye Emerson.

Everyone had a wonderful time.

LETTERS
FROM GINNY CLUB MEMBERS

"I'm feeding Ginnette her bottle three times a day. Do you think that's enough feeding for her? When I get to school I let Ginny take care of Ginnette. I'm bringing Ginnette to school tomorrow."
D. D., Whitehaven, Tenn.

"Ginny is my favorite. And my whole family thinks Ginny is wonderful. Their isn't enough words to tell how wonderful Ginny is."
J. F., Alhambra, Calif.

"Every girl I knew owned a Ginny doll. Then, I got one too. Why don't you make some medical supplies for Ginny? My Ginny doll had a bad case of scarlet fever the other day and almost died."
A. L. B., New York City

1956

Hi...I'm Ginny

Fashion Leader in Doll Society

See my
brand new clothes,
furniture and accessories

VOGUE DOLLS, INC.

Courtesy of Vogue

Unfitted Travel Case — Pink metal and wood case — tapered design.
No. 6864................$6.00

Ginny's Parasol — assorted colors.
No. 6833................$1.00

Doll House and Dog House
White Colonial type — 4 colors — die cut — heavy corrugated — easily assembled.
No. 6926....................$6.00

Gym Set
Swing, slide and glider — sturdy hard-wood, steel and chain construction — easily assembled.
No. 6925....................$8.00

HI-FI FASHIONS

** Shortie Pajama
No. 6221 — $1.00

* OUTFIT ONLY

★ Ginnette Outfit to Match

Ginny's Bed
No. 6910
Bed Only $2.00
No. 6912 Dream Cozy
Set $2.00

* Red Challis Nightgown
No. 6222 — $1.00

* Ginny's Wardrobe
No. 6922 — $3.00

* Cotton Print
Housecoat
No. 6224 — $1.00

" Nitey
and Peignoir
No. 6223 — $2.00

Ginny's Rocking Chair
No. 6914 — $2.00

TO GINNY'S LITTLE MOTHERS...

Ginny and Ginnette in one of their many matching outfits

I know you'll have lots of fun playing with Ginny. Her clothes are made just for her . . . and are designed with the same careful attention to quality and style as your clothes are. Look through all the pictures of Ginny in her very latest fashions . . . she has outfits for every occasion — (and some of them match her baby sister Ginnette's).

Ginny walks, sits, stands, sleeps and comes in bangs or braids in blonde, brunette or auburn wigs of a specially blended hair.

Ginny is made of unbreakable plastic and her walking mechanism is unconditionally guaranteed . . . you'll love her for years and years.

Jennie H Graves
President

VOGUE DOLLS, INC., 33 Ship Ave., Medford 55, Mass.

1956

Party Package
Contains Ginny in panties, shoes and socks, two outfits (assorted materials and styles); note paper, hat, gloves, shoes, Club membership certificate and pin, Club News, and Ginny portrait.
No. 6859................$5.00

SEPARATE COATS

Navy Coat, Hat, Pocketbook
No. 6180 — $1.50

Check Coat, Hat, Pocketbook
No. 6181 — $1.50

Plastic Raincoat & Hood Matching Bag & Umbrella
No. 6182 — $2.00

Velvet Coat, Hat, Pocketbook
No. 6183 — $2.50

Ginny's Pup
No. 6831 — $2.00

Felt Coat, Velvet Headband, Pocketbook
No. 6185 — $2.00

White Fur Coat, Beret, Muff
No. 6184 — $3.00

Borgana Coat, Beret, Muff
No. 6186 — $2.50

Fitted Wardrobe Trunk — Pink metal and wood case with drawer and hangers — includes Ginny in Party Dress and 4 complete outfits.
No. 6862........$10.00

Fitted Wardrobe Trunk. Pink wooden case includes Ginny and two complete outfits.
No. 6860.......$6.00

Fitted Vacation Wardrobe Case. Pink metal and wood case with hangers and drawers — includes Ginny in bedtime outfit and 5 complete outfits.
No. 6865...........$15.00

Fitted Trousseau Chest

Pink and white hardwood construction with swing-up trays; includes Ginny in Bride Outfit and 5 complete additional outfits, plus fur coat and hat, raincoat and umbrella, and many accessories.

No. 6866......................................$29.95

ADDITIONAL ACCESSORIES

No.		
6225	Raincape..................	$ .50
6226	Separate Blouses.........	.75
6227	Separate Skirts..........	.75
6230	Budget Dresses..........	1.00
6231	Beach Roll..............	1.00
6822	Headband and Matching Gloves.................	.25
6836	Bracelet, Beads, Bag Set .	.25
6840	Miniature Suitcase with Mirror, Comb, Nitey, Robe, Slippers.........	1.00
6843	Shoes and Socks........	.25
6844	6 Coat Hangers..........	.25
6847	Ice Skates..............	.60
6848	Roller Skates..........	.60
6851	4 Assorted Plastic Eyeglasses.................	1.00
6854	Wigs—Blonde, Brunette or Auburn in Bangs or Braids	1.00
6870	Metal Stands...........	.50
6917	Quilted and Bound Puff..	.75

1956

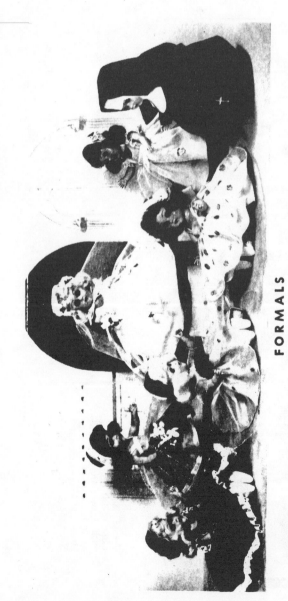

FORMALS

| Dressed Doll No. 6060 Outfit Only No. 6160 | Dressed Doll No. 6061 Outfit Only No. 6161 | Dressed Doll No. 6062 Outfit Only No. 6162 | Dressed Doll No. 6064 Outfit Only No. 6164 | Dressed Doll No. 6063 Outfit Only No. 6163 | Dressed Doll No. 6065 Outfit Only No. 6165 |

DRESSED DOLL $5.00   OUTFIT ONLY $3.00   NUN Dressed Doll Only, No. 6092 (Separate outfit not available)

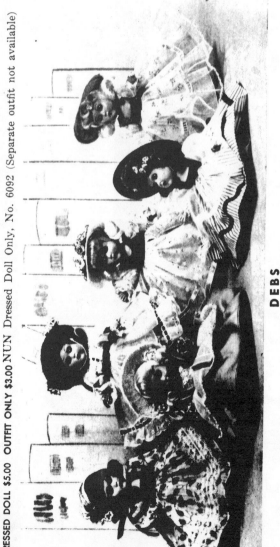

DEBS

| Dressed Doll No. 6070 Outfit Only No. 6170 | Dressed Doll No. 6071 Outfit Only No. 6171 | Dressed Doll No. 6072 Outfit Only No. 6172 | ★Dressed Doll No. 6073 Outfit Only No. 6173 | Dressed Doll No. 6074 Outfit Only No. 6174 | Dressed Doll No. 6075 Outfit Only No. 6175 |

DRESSED DOLL $6.00.............................OUTFIT ONLY $4.00

★ Ginnette Outfit to Match

KINDER CROWD

Dressed Doll No. 6021 Outfit Only No. 6121	★ Dressed Doll No. 6022 Outfit Only No. 6122	Dressed Doll No. 6023 Outfit Only No. 6123	Dressed Doll No. 6024 Outfit Only No. 6124	Dressed Doll No. 6025 Outfit Only No. 6125	Dressed Doll No. 6026 Outfit Only No. 6126

★ Ginnette Outfit to Match   DRESSED DOLL $3.50 . . . . OUTFIT ONLY $1.50

GYM KIDS

Dressed Doll No. 6027 Outfit Only No. 6127	Dressed Doll No. 6028 Outfit Only No. 6128	★ Dressed Doll No. 6029 Outfit Only No. 6129	Dressed Doll No. 6030 Outfit Only No. 6130	Dressed Doll No. 6031 Outfit Only No. 6131	Dressed Doll No. 6032 Outfit Only No. 6132

DRESSED DOLL $3.50 . . . . OUTFIT ONLY $1.50

★ Ginnette Outfit to Match

MERRY MOPPETS

Dressed Doll No. 6033 Outfit Only No. 6133	Dressed Doll No. 6034 Outfit Only No. 6134	Dressed Doll No. 6035 Outfit Only No. 6135	Dressed Doll No. 6036 Outfit Only No. 6136	Dressed Doll No. 6037 Outfit Only No. 6137	Dressed Doll No. 6038 Outfit Only No. 6138

DRESSED DOLL $4.00 . . . . OUTFIT ONLY $2.00

No. 6921 Table and Two Chairs $3.00

PLAY TIME

Dressed Doll No. 6051 Outfit Only No. 6151	Dressed Doll No. 6052 Outfit Only No. 6152	Dressed Doll No. 6053 Outfit Only No. 6153	Dressed Doll No. 6054 Outfit Only No. 6154	Dressed Doll No. 6055 Outfit Only No. 6155	Dressed Doll No. 6056 Outfit Only No. 6156

DRESSED DOLL $4.50 . . . . OUTFIT ONLY $2.50

1956

Matching Pearls for Ginny and Child.
No. 6834 . . . . . $2.00

Ginny's engraved Golden Locket and Chain.
No. 6835 . . . . . $1.00

TINY MISS

Dressed Doll No. 6039 Outfit Only No. 6139	Dressed Doll No. 6040 Outfit Only No. 6140	Dressed Doll No. 6041 Outfit Only No. 6141	Dressed Doll No. 6042 Outfit Only No. 6142	★ Dressed Doll No. 6043 Outfit Only No. 6143	Dressed Doll No. 6044 Outfit Only No. 6144

DRESSED DOLL $4.00 . . . . OUTFIT ONLY $2.00

★ Ginnette Outfit to Match

FUN TIME

Dressed Doll No. 6045 Outfit Only No. 6145	Dressed Doll No. 6046 Outfit Only No. 6146	★ Dressed Doll No. 6047 Outfit Only No. 6147	★ Dressed Doll No. 6048 Outfit Only No. 6148	★ Dressed Doll No. 6049 Outfit Only No. 6149	Dressed Doll No. 6050 Outfit Only No 6150

DRESSED DOLL $4.50 . . . . OUTFIT ONLY $2.50

★ Ginnette Outfit to Match

HAPPY BIRTHDAY TO GINNY AND GINNETTE: In 1956 a special set of party papers was
available in honor of Ginny and Ginnette. It was marketed by PAKAY, a division
of the Gibson Greeting Card Company, and consisted of napkins (shown below), plates
cups and table covers. It was imprinted "HAPPY BIRTHDAY Ginny and Ginnette" and
the main picture was the party scene with three dolls around the table with Sparkie,
the pup, watching. The tablecloths had other pictures of the dolls and the paper
cups had a drawing of Ginny with her pup. What fun little girls must have had
when it was birthday time for them.

TRUE STORIES about GINNY   (Reprinted from January 1958 GINNY CLUB NEWS)

One of the Vogue dealers tells this cute story: A small girl of about six kept
coming into the store buying outfits and accessories for Ginny, but she did not buy
Ginny. The saleslady thought it rather strange, as the little girl did not have a
Ginny doll. She asked her why she was buying outfits when she did not have a doll.
Her reply was, "I expect Ginny for Christmas. When Mummy expects a baby, she always
buys clothes for her before the baby arrives, so that's what I am doing." We know
that she did receive her Ginny for Christmas.

Mr. X in the Vogue office went to see his little granddaughter one weekend. She was
thrilled when he gave her a Ginny booklet and went next door to show it to her friend.
In a short time the little girl came home sobbing as though her heart would break. The
little friend had taken the booklet and would not give it back as she wanted to pick
out new outfits for her Ginny. To stop the crying, Grandpa had to go over and get
the catalog.

GINNY'S PINK CLOUD APARTMENTS, special display at the Doll Shop, SANTA'S VILLAGE, Sky Forest, CA 1957

1956 department store display. Wouldn't it be heaven for collectors to find such a well stocked shop today? There are dozens of boxed outfits and dressed dolls in the background. Furniture and accessories for both Ginny and Ginnette can be seen in the case in the foreground. Strombecker blond wooden furniture is prominent in the case to the far left. Above this are some Ginny items on sale for 99¢. On top of the counter to the right is a prominent display of GINNY'S 12 star plan; a new Ginny outfit every month for a whole year. The certificate came boxed to the recipient and is reproduced on the next page in its original size.

Vogue photo

109

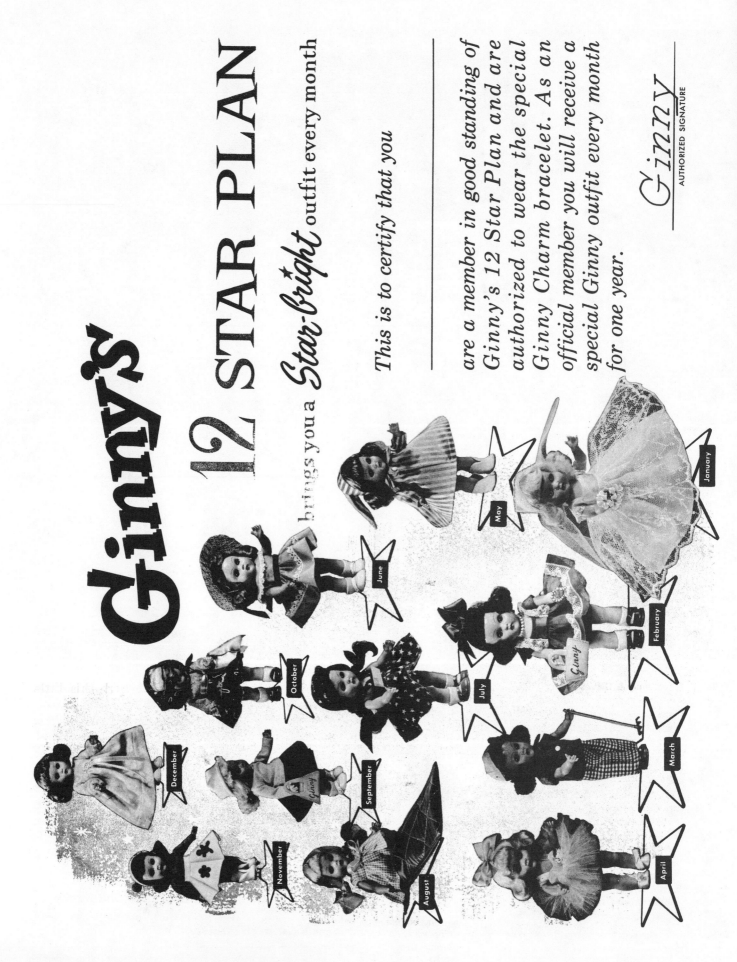

Ginny's 12 STAR PLAN

brings you a Star-bright outfit every month

This is to certify that you

are a member in good standing of Ginny's 12 Star Plan and are authorized to wear the special Ginny Charm bracelet. As an official member you will receive a special Ginny outfit every month for one year.

Ginny
AUTHORIZED SIGNATURE

**GINNY'S
GYM SET**

No. 7925
$8.00

The Vogue Dolls' Family

The famous Ginny, her baby sister Ginnette and their big sister Jill, represent the finest dolls available anywhere . . . at any price. Always insist on these original creations; they are the only names that bear the label of Vogue Dolls, Inc., Fashion Leaders in Doll Society.

We are sorry we cannot sell to individuals direct from our factory, but at your favorite Vogue Dolls dealer you will find a complete selection of all Ginny, Ginnette and Jill outfits and accessories.

Jennie H Graves
President
VOGUE DOLLS, INC.
33 Ship Ave., Medford 55, Mass.

Courtesy of Vogue   Printed in U.S.A.

Ginny · Ginnette
and *Jill*
and their beautiful clothes
for 1957

Fashion Leaders in Doll Society

1957

GINNY'S ACCESSORIES

STYLE NO.		PRICE
7225	Raincape with Hood	$ .60
7226	Separate Blouses	.75
7227	Separate Skirts	.75
7228	Petticoats	.75
7230	Budget Dresses	1.00
7231	Beach Roll Set	1.00
7822	Headband & Gloves	.25
7831	Ginny's Puppy	2.00
7833	Parasol	1.00
7834	Matching Pearl Set	2.00
7835	Locket & Chain	1.00
7836	Beads, Bracelet & Bag	.25
7840	Miniature Suitcase	1.00
7842	Slippers & Sandals	.25
7843	Boxed Shoes & Socks	.25
7844	Six Coat Hangers	.25
7847	Ice Skates	.60
7848	Roller Skates	.60
7849	Rain Bonnet & Boots	.60
7850	Life Jacket & Fins	.60
7851	Eyeglasses, 4 Assorted	1.00
7854	Saran Wigs	1.00
7870	Metal Stands	.60
7917	Quilted Puff	.75

HI, I'M
Ginny

You'll have lots of fun playing with Ginny; she's only 8 inches tall and she sits, stands, kneels, sleeps and is unconditionally guaranteed to walk for as long as you own her.

Ginny is available in three Saran hair styles: braids, bangs or ponytail in brunette, auburn or blonde. And look at all her beautiful clothes and accessories! Ginny is indeed the Fashion Leader in Doll Society!

To be assured of the finest quality always insist on the original GINNY, and her own special outfits and accessories . . . the original creations of Vogue Dolls, Inc. Ginny dressed in panties, shoes and socks is only $2.00.

The best loved dolls in all America are Ginny, Ginnette and Jill. You'll be proud to have three such beautiful dolls as Ginny, Ginnette and Jill in your home as your constant playmates and companions.

As you look through this little book, you will see all the beautiful clothes and accessories that are made especially for Ginny, Ginnette and Jill . . . many of their outfits match each other. Their clothes are custom made with loving care in every detail. Accessories especially designed for these three wonderful dolls will give you many happy hours of play.

This is the Vogue Doll family . . . the Fashion Leaders in Doll Society

Dressed — No. 7021
Outfit — No. 7121

Dressed — No. 7022
Outfit — No. 7122

Dressed — No. 7027
Outfit — No. 7127

Dressed — No. 7028
Outfit — No. 7128

WARDROBE
No. 7922
$3.00

Dressed — No. 7023
Outfit — No. 7123

Dressed — No. 7024
Outfit — No. 7124*

Dressed — No. 7029
Outfit — No. 7129*

Dressed — No. 7030
Outfit — No. 7130

CHEST OF DRAWERS
No. 7920
$3.00

Dressed — No. 7025
Outfit — No. 7125

Dressed — No. 7026
Outfit — No. 7126*†

Dressed — No. 7031
Outfit — No. 7131

Dressed — No. 7032
Outfit — No. 7132

Dressed Doll — $3.50 • Outfit Only — $1.50
*Matching Ginnette Outfit †Matching Jill Outfit

Dressed Doll — $3.50 • Outfit Only — $1.50
*Matching Ginnette Outfit

Dressed — No. 7033
Outfit — No. 7133*

Dressed — No. 7034
Outfit — No. 7134

Dressed — No. 7039
Outfit — No. 7139

Dressed — No. 7040
Outfit — No. 7140

GINNY'S YOUTH BED
No. 7910
$2.00

Dressed — No. 7035
Outfit — No. 7135

Dressed — No. 7036
Outfit — No. 7136

Dressed — No. 7041
Outfit — No. 7141

Dressed — No. 7042
Outfit — No. 7142*†

GINNY'S DREAM COZY BED SET
No. 7912
$2.00

Dressed — No. 7037
Outfit — No. 7137

Dressed — No. 7038
Outfit — No. 7138

Dressed — No. 7043
Outfit — No. 7143†

Dressed — No. 7044
Outfit — No. 7144

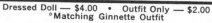

Dressed Doll — $4.00 • Outfit Only — $2.00
*Matching Ginnette Outfit

Dressed Doll — $4.00 • Outfit Only — $2.00
*Matching Ginnette Outfit †Matching Jill Outfit

1957

No. 7180
Coat and Hat — $1.50

No. 7181
Coat and Hat — $1.50

Dressed
No. 7091
$4.50

Outfit
No. 7191
$2.50

Dressed Only
No. 7092 — $5.00

No. 7182 — Coat
Umbrella, Bag — $2.00

No. 7183
Coat and Hat — $2.50

Nighty and Slippers
Outfit Only
No. 7221 — $1.00

Red Flannel Night Shirt
and Cap — Outfit Only
No. 7222 — $1.00

Ginny as shown
$2.00

No. 7184
Coat, Hat, Muff — $3.00

No. 7185
Coat and Hat — $2.00*

3 Piece Pajama Set
Outfit Only
No. 7223 — $2.00

Housecoat
Outfit Only
No. 7224 — $1.00

*Matching Ginnette Coat

FITTED WARDROBE CASE

Made of pink wood — contains Ginny and two complete outfits.
No. 7860 $6.00

No. 7186 — Borgana Coat,
Hat, Muff — $2.50

No. 7187
Car Coat — $2.00

TABLE AND CHAIRS
No. 7921 — $3.00

FITTED WARDROBE TRUNK

Pink metal and wood — contains dressed Ginny plus three complete outfits and accessories.
No. 7862 $10.00
UNFITTED
No. 7864 $4.00

PARTY PACKAGE

Contains Ginny, two outfits, Ginny Club Kit, assorted accessories.
No. 7859 $5.00

ROCKING CHAIR
No. 7914 — $2.00

FITTED TRAVEL TRUNK

Wood covered with pink and white stitched metal — contains dressed Ginny, plus three specially selected complete outfits and many accessories.
No. 7865 $15.00

GINNY'S APRON SET

Matching "Happy Birthday" aprons for Ginny and her mother.
No. 7837 $2.00

Dressed — No. 7045
Outfit — No. 7145

Dressed — No. 7046
Outfit — No. 7146

Dressed — No. 7051
Outfit — No. 7151

Dressed — No. 7052
Outfit — No. 7152

FITTED TROUSSEAU CHEST

Pink and white hardwood — includes Ginny in Bride Outfit, five additional outfits, fur coat, raincoat, umbrella, many accessories.
No. 7866 $29.95

Dressed — No. 7047
Outfit — No. 7147

Dressed — No. 7048
Outfit — No. 7148*

Dressed — No. 7053
Outfit — No. 7153

Dressed — No. 7054
Outfit — No. 7154

Dressed — No. 7049
Outfit — No. 7149*

Dressed — No. 7050
Outfit — No. 7150

Dressed — No. 7055
Outfit — No. 7155*

Dressed — No. 7056
Outfit — No. 7156

Dressed Doll — $4.50 • Outfit Only — $2.50
*Matching Ginnette Outfit

Dressed Doll — $4.50 • Outfit Only — $2.50
*Matching Ginnette Outfit

Dressed — No. 7060
Outfit — No. 7160

Dressed — No. 7061
Outfit — No. 7161

Dressed — No. 7070
Outfit — No. 7170

Dressed — No. 7073
Outfit — No. 7173

"GADABOUT" CASE

Gayly colored case for carrying Ginny, "magic-fold" window, separate accessory compartment.

No. 7863 $5.00

Dressed — No. 7062
Outfit — No. 7162†

Dressed — No. 7063
Outfit — No. 7163

Dressed — No. 7071
Outfit — No. 7171

Dressed — No. 7074
Outfit — No. 7174

KNIT KIT
Yarn, instructions and buttons for three cardigan sweaters and three cuddle caps for Ginny, Ginnette and Jill — knit one for each or 3 for one.

Dressed — No. 7064
Outfit — No. 7164†

Dressed — No. 7065
Outfit — No. 7165

Dressed — No. 7072
Outfit — No. 7172

Dressed — No. 7075
Outfit — No. 7175

No. 7869
$1.00

Dressed Doll — $5.00 • Outfit Only — $3.00
†Matching Jill Outfit

Dressed Doll — $6.00
Outfit Only — $4.00

Dressed Doll — $7.00
Outfit Only — $5.00

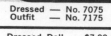

1957

1958 CHRISTMAS CARD; inside verse:

"Six little Vogue Dolls
Brim full of cheer
Wish you a Merry Christmas
and a Happy New Year"

Signed in handwriting:

Jennie Graves   Virginia Carlson

ARTIST: Marion Quimby

All cards courtesy of
Jennie Davis who as a
Vogue home sewer re-
ceived them for the
four years she worked
for Vogue, 1955-1958

Original cards were in
full color and do not
reproduce perfectly
in black and white

1957 CHRISTMAS CARD; inside verse:

"Three Little Vogue Dolls.
trimming the tree
To make Christmas Merry
for you and for me
Getting ready for Santa
brim full of cheer
And wishing you girls
a HAPPY NEW YEAR"
Signed:
"Ginny, Ginnette and Jill"

I'm Ginny

I'm Jimmy

I'm Jill

The Vogue Doll Family

I'm Ginny

I'm Ginnette

Their fabulous clothes and accessories for 1958

Fashion Leaders in Doll Society

What's your name? Isn't it fun to meet like this? I just know we're going to have good times playing together...tea parties with all our friends (I can wear my new organdy pinafore) . . . skating or skiing in my beautiful sport outfits . . . and just wait till you see me in my cowgirl suit. I have boots and even carry a gun! But let's turn the pages together and look at ALL my wonderful new clothes and accessories.

Ginny is 8 inches tall. She sleeps, sits, stands, kneels and walks. Available in three hair styles . . . bangs, ponytail or braids, in brunette, auburn or blonde.

Dressed in panties, shoes and socks — $2.00

I'm Ginny

3690 $2.00 To wear yourself — a Ginny Ginnette and Jill charm bracelet.

1561 $1.00 New look for Ginny — three styles, each in three colors. Blonde, brunette, auburn.

Vogue Dolls for gift occasions

For birthdays, Christmas or any gift occasion, give the gift that will bring endless joy for years to come — give a Vogue Doll.

When purchasing their outfits and accessories — or supplementing an already growing wardrobe — make your selection from the exciting new collection of fabulous fashions for 1958.

Every little girl loves a Vogue Doll!

Vogue Dolls and their accessories are at your favorite store

You will find a complete line of Vogue Dolls, their outfits and accessories at better stores throughout the country.

Always insist on these original creations bearing the label, "Vogue Dolls, Inc., Fashion Leaders in Doll Society."

We are sorry but they cannot be purchased directly from our factory.

VOGUE DOLLS, INC.
33 Ship Ave., Medford 55, Mass.

Courtesy of Vogue

1500 25¢ Pretty little shoes and socks in assorted colors.

116

Dressed 1165 $5.00   Outfit 1365 $3.00
Ginny as a bridesmaid in beautiful blue tulle with whispery under-skirt of blue taffeta. She wears a circlet of flowers, carries a bouquet.

Outfit 1367 $3.00
Ginny's snow white, real bunny fur is beautiful and cozy warm. Her perky little hat in matching bunny fur.

Outfit 1300 $1.00†
Here's Ginny, cute as a button in her cotton jersey leotard and tiny satin ballet slippers. Her leotard in pink, black or red.

Outfit 1326 $1.50
For dress-up Ginny wears this aqua coat with gold and black flower print. Her hat, black velveteen faced with matching print.

Dressed 1151 $4.50   Outfit 1351 $2.50
Ginny in her roller-skating skirt of swirling pink felt that's silk screened to spell "Ginny". Matching cap, black leotard, skates.

Dressed 1169 $5.00
Ginny dressed in her nun's habit of black. Gold-like cross hangs from the waist.

Dressed 1180 $6.00   Outfit 1380 $4.00
Bewitching Country Fair gown in colorful print with sheer blouse and black basque bodice. Hat and bag in mauve straw.

Outfit 1302 $1.00
Pretty flowery housecoat with full, full skirt. Sparkling white cotton splashed with roses and edged with delicate white lace.

Outfit 1303 $1.00
Let's play! And Ginny can wear her princess dress of crispy, colorful cotton. The skirt is full and flary and edged in scalloped rick rack.

Dressed 1150 $4.50   Outfit 1350 $2.50
Ballet is fun! Here Ginny wears a frilly white tulle costume with silver lamé bodice. Her ballet slippers and flower wreath are pink.

Dressed 1181 $6.00   Outfit 1381 $4.00
Isn't Ginny beautiful in her full length party pinafore? Fantasy green with lace edged organdy apron. Her hat a natural straw.

Dressed 1190 $7.00   Outfit 1390 $5.00
Ginny, sweet as can be in frothy white organdy and radiant red velvet elegantly edged with lace. Hat and pouch to match.

Outfit 1304 $1.00
This is Ginny's little shirtmaker dress . . . crisp and new as Spring in sparkling, colorful cotton with convertible collar and full skirt.

Outfit 1305 $1.00
What fun when Ginny wears her new yoke dress! The skirt falls to gentle fullness from the shoulders, and the colors are so bright and gay.

Dressed 1164 $5.00   Outfit 1364 $3.00†
Ginny's beautiful bridal gown of gleaming white satin and tulle. She wears a chapel length veil and carries a bouquet of flowers.

† Matching Jill outfit

Dressed 1140 $4.00   Outfit 1340 $2.00
How Ginny loves her swirling blue corduroy skirt, sheer white top and black felt bolero jacket. Her cap is black felt with lace trim.

Dressed 1130 $4.00   Outfit 1330 $2.00†
The gayest little dress we know, this bright red cotton sailor with white trim, white satin tie. Her hat, white felt banded with red.

Outfit 1359 $2.50
Ginny's toasty warm coat is made of cloud-light beige dynel and lined with crispy taffeta. Close fitting headband to match.

Dressed 1160 $5.00   Outfit 1360 $3.00
Beautiful navy linen coat over a cotton dress of red and blue print. Coat is lined with matching print. Flower-pot hat in white straw.

Dressed 1163 $5.00   Outfit 1363 $3.00
Pretty little princess dress of bright red velveteen with lace from shoulders to hemline. Her hat, layer upon layer of white tulle.

Outfit 1345 $2.00
This is Ginny's navy felt Regulation Coat . . . brass buttoned and trimmed with red eagle emblem. Her hat is navy, her purse is white.

Outfit 1346 $2.00
For rainy days Ginny wears this pretty, plastic, hooded raincoat. She carries a matching purse and workable umbrella.

Dressed 1161 $5.00   Outfit 1361 $3.00
Ginny says "I like lollypops and ice-cream cones" on this skirt of pale pink felt. With it, a matching felt jacket and pink hat.

Dressed 1162 $5.00   Outfit 1362 $3.00
Very special party dress has white nylon embroidered skirt, black velveteen bodice, pink sash. Black straw trimmed with pink.

Dressed 1120 $3.50   Outfit 1320 $1.50†
Beige twill jodhpurs for riding or relaxing. With them a colorful print blouse, bright collar pin, brown belt and brown boots.

Dressed 1152 $4.50   Outfit 1352 $2.50
Ginny struts in her drum majorette costume of white cotton with sparkly gold braid trim. Gold panties, visor hat, baton.

Dressed 1153 $4.50   Outfit 1353 $2.50
Here we see Ginny ready for underwater exploring in a white suit, orange life jacket, face mask and fins. Towel and pail are for fun!

Dressed 1134 $4.00   Outfit 1334 $2.00
This is Ginny's green and white gingham, trimmed ever-so-daintily with white eyelet embroidery. Her big hat is natural straw.

Dressed 1133 $4.00   Outfit 1333 $2.00
For birthday parties a pretty, pretty yellow flocked taffeta, lace trimmed and tied with satin. Matching bonnet trimmed with lace.

Dressed 1121 $3.50   Outfit 1321 $1.50†
This is one of Ginny's favorites! Bright red Capri pants and matching harlequin pattern overblouse. Her glasses are white plastic.

Dressed 1154 $4.50   Outfit 1354 $2.50††
Ski suit for freezy-cold days in aqua cotton with button-up jacket, separate pants, fur trimmed hood and mitts. Skiis, poles included.

Dressed 1155 $4.50   Outfit 1355 $2.50†
Ginny's beautiful coral skating dress gleams with silver threads. Her matching hat sports a real feather. Skates included.

Dressed 1114 $3.50   Outfit 1314 $1.50†
For warm summer days Ginny wears a dress of primrose yellow cotton. The skirt is full, the neckline and sleeves edged with lace.

Dressed 1137 $4.00   Outfit 1337 $2.00
Ginny in white cotton organdy trimmed with black rick rack and sashed with black velveteen. Straw hat has red flower.

1690 $2.00 For Ginny and her "mother" — matching pearl beads and bracelet.

Dressed 1156 $4.50   Outfit 1356 $2.50
Here we see Ginny in a silver fringed white felt cowgirl outfit. Bright shirt, white felt hat, silver cuffs and boots and toting a gun.

†† Matching Jill and Ginnette c

Dressed 1131 $4.00   Outfit 1331 $2.00
Here Ginny wears a crisp white nurse's uniform and just-like-real nurse's cap. In her hand she carries a hot water bottle.

Dressed 1138 $4.00   Outfit 1338 $2.00†
Pretty little sleeveless cotton in pale pink with a bouquet of flowers at the waist. Matching pink jersey shrug and hat of pink straw.

† Matching Jill outfit

Dressed 1139 $4.00   Outfit 1339 $2.00†
Ginny in trim, slim slacks of tartan plaid. The white bulky knit sweater bright with brass buttons. On her head a white straw bowler.

1565 $1.00 Personalized miniature suitcase with comb, mirror, slippers, nightie and robe, all in assorted colors.

Dressed 1116 $3.50   Outfit 1316 $1.50*
A-gardening we will go! And Ginny can wear her pretty rose play-apron and matching pants. She even has her own watering can!

Dressed 1117 $3.50   Outfit 1317 $1.50†
All ready for "Coke"** and Ginny wears a white cotton shirt and blue denim jeans. Her glasses are white plastic.

Dressed 1110 $3.50   Outfit 1310 $1.50†
How Ginny loves a sundress! This one is crispy white polished cotton banded with black on the skirt and tied with a bow on the shoulders.

Dressed 1115 $3.50   Outfit 1315 $1.50†
Red and white candy striped cotton, gay as a summer day with swirling skirt, lace edged sleeves and sparkling white belt to circle the waist.

1501 25¢ pr. Ginny's sandals and slippers come in two styles each, in assorted colors.

Dressed 1118 $3.50   Outfit 1318 $1.50†
Ginny has fun-times when she dresses in her Ivy League striped Bermudas, black belt, red jersey shirt and matching socks.

Dressed 1119 $3.50   Outfit 1319 $1.50
When the air is nippy Ginny feels cuddly-warm in her aqua knit "Ginny" sweater and skirt of white polished cotton.

Dressed 1112 $3.50   Outfit 1312 $1.50†
What a sweet little cotton this is! Every line so new and smart. The blouse is aqua . . . the skirt white with aqua flower print.

Dressed 1113 $3.50   Outfit 1313 $1.50†
Pretty as a picture, this red and white polka dot dress has a flaring skirt, black belt and black ribbon beading on sleeves and neckline.

1553 75¢ pr. Ginny's rain bonnet and boots in transparent plastic.

1958

1860 $3.00 Ginny's pink vanity table with matching bench has lift-up mirror and plastic comb.

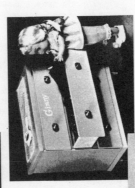

1852 $2.00 Rocking Chair for Ginny. Comes in pink wood and really rocks.

1861 $3.00 Ginny's round table and two matching chairs in pink wood.

1862 $3.00 Ginny's wardrobe is pink painted wood with clothes rod and clothes hangers. Personalized with Ginny's name.

1880 $4.00 Ginny's three drawer dresser is pink and printed with Ginny's name. Comb, mirror and dresser Scarf.

1890 $8.00 Ginny's Gym Set is gay and colorful and printed with Ginny's name.

1560 $1.00 Four piece Beach Roll Set has bathing suit, towel, pail and beach roll.

1502 25¢ Ginny's handbag, beads and bracelet set in gay assorted colors.

1535 60¢ Cuddly felt mittens and ear muff set, in gay assorted colors.

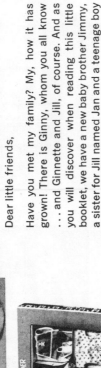

Dear little friends,

Have you met my family? My, how it has grown! There is Ginny, whom you all know . . . and Ginnette and Jill, of course. And as you will discover when reading this little booklet, we have a new baby brother Jimmy, a sister for Jill named Jan and a teenage boy whom we call Jeff.

And because I know how much you love your dolls and want them all beautifully dressed, I again give you my pledge to maintain the very highest quality possible . . . and to continue to bring you the newest, most exciting fashions ever designed.

May you always have happy hours with your family of Vogue Dolls.

Sincerely,

Jennie H Graves
President

1958

1745 $7.00 Fitted wardrobe case in pale pink wood. Contains Ginny dressed in shoes, socks, panties and petticoat plus three separate outfits.

1760 $15.00 Fitted Travel Trunk in wood, covered with pink and white stitched metal. Ginny dressed in party pinafore with four separate outfits and numerous accessories.

1750 $10.00 Week-ender Package contains Ginny dressed in pretty party outfit and four other ensembles.

1850 $2.00 Ginny's Bed. Comes in pink wood, imprinted with Ginny's name.
1851 $2.00 Dream Cozy Bed Set has pillow, pillow case, two contour sheets and spread.

1660 $1.00 Golden heart shaped locket and matching chain.

1568 $1.00 Ginny's eye glasses come in assorted colors — four to a set.

now you and **Ginny** can dress- alike

it exciting! Eight of Ginny's newest, most fashionable outfits are interpretations of nationally famous Vogue Patterns for children. Now you and Ginny can have that "dress-alike" look!

Just turn the following pages until you find the same Ginny outfits that are illustrated here with the matching Vogue Patterns ...you'll see a complete description of colors and fabrics used for Ginny's own identical fashions.

And be sure to ask mommy to buy your "dress-alike" Vogue Pattern soon! Available only in pattern departments.

Vogue Pattern 2748
Ginny Outfit 1301

Vogue Pattern 2771
Ginny Outfit 1336

Vogue Pattern 2741
Ginny Outfit 1341

Vogue Pattern 2765
Ginny Outfit 1311

Vogue Pattern 2755
Ginny Outfit 1332

Vogue Pattern 2766
Ginny Outfit 1325

Vogue Pattern 2757
Ginny Outfit 1358

Vogue Pattern 2786
Ginny Outfit 1335

1566 $1.00 Ginny's personalized parasol that really works comes in pretty assorted colors.

1532 60¢ pr. Ginny's white suedine roller skates really roll.

1531 60¢ pr. Ginny's ice skates in white suedine.

1958

1567 $1.00 Colorful life jacket, swim fins and face mask.

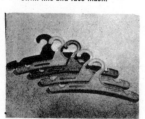

1503 25¢ Personalized coat hangers in colorful molded plastic. Set of 5.

1591 $2.00 Ginny's little play-puppy with colorful plaid blanket coat.

1552 75¢ Separate felt skirt in a gay array of colors.

1534 60¢ Ginny's school bag in colorful plaid plastic. Golden play watch has printed face.

1590 $2.00 Matching birthday aprons for Ginny and her little mother in white with pink designs.

1504 25¢ Ginny's personalized headband and matching gloves in a gay array of colors.

1530 60¢ Plastic hooded raincape in gay rainbow colors.

1551 75¢ Separate ruffled petticoats from Ginny's Petticoat Lane come in assorted fabrics and colors.

1550 75¢ Pretty little separate blouses in assorted styles, fabrics and colors.

Dressed 1256 $4.50   Outfit 1456 $2.50
British Islander. Red plaid kilt, lace jabot and black felt doublet. Sporran, tam-o'-shanter and trim white spats.

Dressed 1255 $4.50   Outfit 1455 $2.50
Israelian. Colorful striped dress with bright metallic banding on bodice, sleeves and skirt. White veil, golden chains, Star of David.

Dressed 1254 $4.50   Outfit 1454 $2.50
Oriental. Pink flowered kimono. Obi sash is jade flower print embroidered with metallic threads. Fan, parasol, slippers, lotus flowers.

Dressed 1257 $4.50   Outfit 1457 $2.50
Hollander. Rich, red and blue striped dress, white lace vestee, embroidered winged cap and apron. Coral necklace with golden bun, wooden klompen.

Dressed 1258 $4.50   Outfit 1458 $2.50
Alaskan. Furry brown pants, parka and hood are accented with touches of white. She wears colorful mukleks on her feet.

Ginny's Costumes from Far-Away Lands

Ginny Doll Family

ISRAELIAN 1455   BRITISH ISLANDER 1456   HOLLANDER 1457
ORIENTAL 1454   ALASKAN 1458
SCANDINAVIAN 1453   HAWAIIAN 1459

Dressed 1253 $4.50   Outfit 1453 $2.50
Scandinavian. Has black skirt, red laced bodice, white blouse and red and white striped apron. Fringed kerchief and flowered cap.

Dressed 1259 $4.50   Outfit 1459 $2.50
Hawaiian. Festive red flower print sarong. A wreath of flowers for her hair. Colorful lei, sandals and surf board.

1959

Courtesy of Vogue

All furniture pieces and accessories of 1958 were also available during 1959.

Dressed 1230 $4.00 Outfit 1430 $2.00 ‡
Wonderful for anytime — Ginny's Emerald green wool felt blazer with patch pockets, Peter Pan collar and pleated skirt. Beanie to match.

1430

Dressed 1231 $4.00 Outfit 1431 $2.00 ‡ ✱
Another of Ginny's party frocks — sheer yellow organdy with nylon petticoat, ribbon beading, lace and satin trim. Imported straw hat.

1431

Dressed 1232 $4.00 Outfit 1432 $2.00 ‡
Ginny's shirtwaist classic in gay blue check with cluster pleated skirt, roll-up sleeves and navy jersey cardigan. Beanie to match.

1432

Outfit 1445 $2.00
Ginny has fun in the rain when she wears her hooded plastic raincoat! She carries a matching tote bag and umbrella that really works.

Outfit 1446 $2.00
Ginny looks glamorous when she wears her white, real bunny fur coat. The perky little hat and muff are a perfect match.

Dressed 1233 $4.00 Outfit 1433 $2.00 ‡
For play-time Ginny loves to wear these blue corduroy slacks and bright red felt jacket. Her straw sailor is trimmed with red ribbons.

Dressed 1234 $4.00 Outfit 1434 $2.00 ‡
Isn't Ginny sweet in her new party dress? Tiny pink check with crispy, stand-out pinafore of white pique. Pink satin bow for her hair.

1433

1434

1445

1446

1450

1451

1452

Dressed 1250 $4.50 Outfit 1450 $2.50 †
Ginny loves to ice skate in her red leotard, swirling white felt skirt and short cropped jacket. She has a headband and skates, too.

Dressed 1252 $4.50 Outfit 1452 $2.50 ††
For freezy-cold days, Ginny wears green wool felt pants and plaid bloused jacket. White earmuff cap, boots, mittens, skis and poles.

Dressed 1251 $4.50 Outfit 1451 $2.50 ††
Ginny goes Western in her Rodeo outfit of Ranch blue twill trimmed with silver and black. Gun and holster set — white hat and boots.

1460

1269

Dressed 1260 $5.00 Outfit 1460 $3.00
Ginny's beautiful bridal gown is gleaming white satin and tulle. She wears a chapel length veil and carries a flower bouquet.

Dressed 1269 $5.00
Ginny dressed in her Nun's habit of black broadcloth. A golden cross hangs from the waist.

Vogue photos

1959

Outfit 1400 $1.00
Ginny's having a slumber party! She chooses these two-piece pajamas in gayly printed crinkle cloth.

Dressed 1210 $3.50   Outfit 1410 $1.50 †
Sailing, anyone? You'll love this jaunty cotton sun dress in red, white and blue with flary skirt, anchor motif and crisp white braid.

Outfit 1401 $1.00
Ginny has fun-times when she wears her navy shorts and colorful blouse fastened with a golden pin. She has sunglasses, too.

Dressed 1211 $3.50   Outfit 1411 $1.50
Our pretty ballerina wears a frilly aqua tulle costume with matching taffeta bodice. Ballet slippers, mask and crown.

Outfit 1402 $1.00
Perky little sunsuit in gay assorted patterns has romper pants and nylon ruffle trim. She has saucy sunglasses and rake.

Dressed 1212 $3.50 Outfit 1412 $1.50 ††
Let's meet for a Coke*! You'll see Ginny in her own jersey sweater, blue denim jeans and golden rimmed sunglasses.

Outfit 1403 $1.00
It's party time — and Ginny looks so sweet in sparkling fabrics with full flary skirt, snowy white lace trim and satin ribbon sash.

Dressed 1213 $3.50 Outfit 1413 $1.50 †††
Look at Ginny! She's wearing a new cropped top of white embroidered cotton and flary skirt of Party pink. Pink pearly headband,

Dressed 1214 $3.50   Outfit 1414 $1.50 ‡
Doesn't Ginny look smart in her new high-waisted, red polished cotton! Collar and cuffs frosted with Venice lace — headband to match.

Dressed 1215 $3.50   Outfit 1415 $1.50 †
A favorite of Ginny's in Bewitching-blue cotton. The yoke and skirt banded with polka dots and white Venice lace. Blue pearly headband.

Outfit 1425 $1.50
A ''must'' for every wardrobe! Ginny's navy felt Regulation coat with brass buttons and Scottie cap. Sparkling white purse.

Outfit 1426 $1.50
Ginny's toasty warm coat is made of cloud-light beige dynel, lined with crispy taffeta. And just imagine, a beret and muff to match!

1959

1960'S

By the sixties, Ginny's heydays were over. Clearly the fifties were her very own heyday, a common expression to denote a period of greatest vigor and success; the word 'hey' goes back to Anglo-Saxon use as an expression of greeting denoting much enthusiasm and happiness.

What were the reasons that spelled a decline for Ginny? It was a new doll called Barbie. She was being produced in the far east at considerably less cost than other dolls and so competition became very keen in the doll industry especially for the companies who were specializing in the small dolls.

However, during this decade Vogue continued to produce Ginny and also introduced several new and larger dolls to their line, including GINNY BABY, WEE IMP, LITTLE IMP, BRICKETTE and a big 36" GINNY walking doll. The big Ginny always carried an 8" one with her and they were dressed in matching outfits with three changes of clothing.

Ginny had some two dozen new togs for 1960 and a number of accessories but the furniture was discontinued. In 1961 more dolls were added to the GINNY DOLL FAMILY including the following: LITTLEST ANGEL, an 11" toddler; BABY DEAR in 12" and 18' sizes; GINNY BABY in 12",16", 18" and 20" sizes; DREAM BABY, a 16" vinyl sculptured hair doll; and BRIKETTE in 16" and 22" sizes. Ginny had only 13 changes of outfits and all accessories were dropped except for replacement wigs and stands. Jeff, Jan and the hard plastic Jill were discontinued.

In 1962 Ginny had 15 new outfits and new dolls introduced were: 25" BABY DEAR ONE; 16" MISS GINNY; and all new JILL, a 10 1/2" teen-aged doll with a durable plastic body and soft vinyl arms and head with rooted hair. Ginnette, Ginny Baby, LittlestAngel and Baby Dear were carried over. This was the first year for the 8" Ginny Baby.

The soft vinyl head with rooted hair was added to Ginny in 1963. The marking impressed on the back was the same as #5: GINNY VOGUE DOLLS, INC. PAT. NO. 2687594, Made in U. S. A. There were 15 new outfits for Ginny. New dolls added include: 8" LI'L DEAR that had the same face as Ginnette with rooted hair and a soft body; 23" TOO DEAR, a cherubic, pudgy two year old version of Baby Dear; and a new 12" teen doll girl friend to Jill named JAN. Baby Dears were continued and were available as moving infants with a Swiss-made mechanism and the Baby Dear One doll was introduced as twins in matching boy and girl outfits. Miss Ginny, Littlest Angel and Ginnette were also available.

The only new dolls offered in 1964 were 'JAMA BABY,'a pajama bag doll and BUNNY HUG, a soft fleece doll but three dolls were produced in a black version. Also, Ginnette, Li'l Imp and four sizes of Ginny Baby. Ginny had 13 new designs. Jan, Li'l Dear and Baby Dear were continued.

In 1965 foam bodied 17" POSY PIXI was new; also 16" LOVE ME LINDA; 10" and 14" ANGEL BABY were added and a 15" MY ANGEL was planned but evidently never marketed. Dolls held over were: Baby Dear, Baby Dear One, Dream Baby, 'Jama Baby, Bunny Hug,Ginnette, Li'l Imp, Too Dear, Miss Ginny and vinyl Jill in a special "HISTORY LAND" series. By this time Ginny was an all vinyl doll and marked GINNY on her head and GINNY, VOGUE DOLLS, INC. on back. She was Ginny #8 and came with five costumes in "Fairytale Land" and nine in "Far-AwayLands".

124

There were no new dolls brought out during 1966 and some of the previous years' dolls were dropped like Posy Pixi, Love Me Linda, Angel Baby, Baby Dear One, Bunny Hug, Ginnette, Too Dear, Miss Ginny and Jill. Still in production were Littlest Angel, Li'l Dear, Dream Baby, two sizes of Baby Dear and three sizes of Ginny Baby. The vinyl Ginny had quite an array of costumes including ten play and party dresses, a nun's habit, eleven in the "Fairytale Land" series and fourteen in the "Far-Away Lands"; these last two series included some attractively costumed pairs of dolls in matching outfits.

STAR BRIGHT, a 19" vinyl toddler, was brought out in 1968, as were also 12" and 15" MISS GINNYS. Baby Dear and Baby Dear-one were remolded with moving eyes. Two sizes of Ginny Babys were offered in both sculptured and rooted hair versions; there were two sizes of Littlest Angel and Baby Dear. Ginnette was continued and Ginny had nine changes of everyday togs and 24 from the "Far-Away Lands" series which this year included ones like the nun, nurse, bride, cowgirl, pilgrim and stewardess.

The year 1969 brought no new dolls but several of the previous year were continued like Littlest Angel, Ginny Baby, 12" Miss Ginny and 15" Miss Ginny Debutante. Also Baby Dear in three sizes and the big 25" Baby Dear-One along with the little Dream Baby which had Ginnette's head. Fitted bassinettes could be purchased for the Baby Dear dolls in different sizes; these were completely lined with taffeta with a full puckered nylon skirt embroidered with dainty flowers and had a taffeta mattress, pillow and coverlet edged in gathered lace. A new package design of white and deep blue boxes was added and dolls like Littlest Angel had several changes of outfits packed in the box. There were also fitted and empty metal trunks with drawers, hangers and travel decals.

This was the last year for American-made Ginnys and she had ten costumes for general wear and twelve in the Far-Away Lands collector series. They continued to be sold in the stores, however, for several years, so it appeared that they were never completely off the market.

Ginny had endured for over four decades, the longest known time of any doll being produced continuously, to the best of my knowledge. Surely this charming miniature doll was not destined to fade away? What plans were being made for her in the years ahead and what was to happen to her in the next decade?

WEE IMP: 8", carrot red haired, green eyed Wee Imp was a special issue of the basic Ginny walker, bending knee doll offered only one year - 1960. She is marked, GINNY but wore a wrist tag designating her as WEE IMP. She wore Ginny's clothes, of course. There were four special outfits that had matching ones for the 11" L'IL IMP (special version of Littlest Angel). At the right is the candy striped pajama set with night cap. Other three outfits were the faded blue jeans with red checked cuffs and matching shirt; the turquoise dotted dress with lace trimmed pinafore; and the blue felt pop-over worn with white tights and jersey top with saucy beret.

The Ginny Doll Family

FASHION LEADERS IN DOLL SOCIETY

A 1960 PRESENTATION OF

Vogue Dolls INC.

33 SHIP AVENUE
MEDFORD 55, MASS.

Vogue Dolls INC.

Hi, I'm Ginny

1960

BASIC DOLL $2.00
I'm 8" tall and can sleep, sit, stand, kneel and walk. I'm available in two hair styles — bangs or braids — in blonde, brunette or auburn. Dressed in panties, shoes and socks.

OUTFIT 1301 $1.00
Ginny takes a stroll in this afternoon dress with gayly checked yoke and flary white skirt. Lace edges the neckline and sleeves.

OUTFIT 1302 $1.00
It's time for school and Ginny wears a colorful cotton dress. The skirt is full and the yoke trimmed prettily at the waist.

OUTFIT 1303 $1.00
Ginny has sweet dreams when she wears these 2-piece pajamas of brightly assorted fabrics.

DRESSED 1110 $3.50
OUTFIT 1310 $1.50
How sweet Ginny looks in her dainty pink checked dress with lace trimmed organdy pie-plate collar and flower motif. Pink plastic headband.

DRESSED 1111 $3.50
OUTFIT 1311 $1.50
There's fun-time ahead for Ginny when she wears her colorful felt jodphurs and long-sleeved white jersey.

DRESSED 1112 $3.50
OUTFIT 1312 $1.50
Ginny looks like a drop of golden sun in white organdy and yellow polished cotton. Frosty lace trims skirt and on the yoke — a flower motif. Pearly yellow headband.

DRESSED 1113 $3.50
OUTFIT 1313 $1.50
Ginny can climb trees in her faded blue denim jeans with red and white checked shirt. Her hat is a natural straw roller.

DRESSED 1114 $3.50
OUTFIT 1314 $1.50
How Ginny loves to dress up in this crisp aqua dress of polished cotton. The striped crop top is prettily edged with white lace.

OUTFIT 1325 $1.50
Ginny doesn't mind the rain at all when she wears her hooded plastic raincoat. She carries a matching tote bag and umbrella that really works!

OUTFIT 1326 $1.50
For Sunday or visiting Ginny loves to wear her scarlet red velveteen coat and hat. She carries a white purse.

OUTFIT 1327 $1.50
When it's freezy cold Ginny is cozy and warm in her snow white bunny fur coat with matching beret and <u>muff.</u>

DRESSED 1130 $4.00
OUTFIT 1330 $2.00
Ginny has a cookout and wears a perky white apron with rooster motif over a sleeveless red and white checked dress. And see her matching white chef's hat!

DRESSED 1131 $4.00
OUTFIT 1331 $2.00
Ginny looks like a French schoolgirl in her blue felt popover trimmed with white braid and red sailboat worn over white jersey leotights. Her matching felt sassy beret sports a pom-pom.

127

| DRESSED 1132 | $4.00 | DRESSED 1133 | $4.00 | DRESSED 1134 | $4.00 | DRESSED 1135 | $4.00 | DRESSED 1150 | $4.50 |
| OUTFIT 1332 | $2.00 | OUTFIT 1333 | $2.00 | OUTFIT 1334 | $2.00 | OUTFIT 1335 | $2.00 | OUTFIT 1350 | $2.50 |

Darling little party dress with lace edged black velveteen yoke and swirling skirt of white taffeta with flower motif. Gauzy bows trim her pink straw hat and she carries her own pink pocketbook.

Bright and gay is Ginny in this lace-edged afternoon dress of cherry-red cotton. Her flower trimmed hat ties on top with a perky satin bow.

Ginny dons a yellow felt hat and carries a yellow handbag when she wears this print dress. Skirt and yoke are smartly trimmed with cotton lace.

Ginny enters the Land of Nod wearing this colorful candy-striped pajama set with full blown top. And doesn't her nite cap look cute? Pink pom-pom slippers.

Here's Ginny sweet in her quaint little white pinafore worn over a turquoise dotted dress. See her matching white bloomers and long cotton stockings?

1960

| DRESSED 1151 | $4.50 | DRESSED 1152 | $4.50 | DRESSED 1160 | $5.00 | DRESSED 1161 | $5.00 | DRESSED only 1169 | $5.00 |
| OUTFIT 1351 | $2.50 | OUTFIT 1352 | $2.50 | OUTFIT 1360 | $3.00 | OUTFIT 1361 | $3.00 | | |

Ginny totes a gun when she wears her gold-fringed red and white cowgirl outfit. Belt and holster, white felt hat and boots complete the Western costume.

Sugar and spice . . . frosty ruffles and rosebuds trim this dainty white organdy frock. Worn with the laciest pantalettes and pink satin slippers. Her hat is white straw with matching trim and pink satin ribbon ties.

Ginny steals the scene in a blue nylon gown daintily frosted with white lace. She carries an old-fashioned nosegay and wears a circlet of blue flowers in her hair.

Here comes the bride in lace-trimmed satin and tulle. Her chapel-length veil is held in place by a pearl crown. Her bouquet — white, of course!

Ginny wears a Nun's habit of black broadcloth. A golden cross hangs from the waist.

Hi, I'm 36" Ginny

I AM
DRESSED 1190
$25.00 PER SET

Ginny loves to romp about in her rugged jeans of faded blue denim. Her classic tailored shirt is red checked with real buttons. On her head is a natural straw roller. In her hand — a matching 8" Ginny.

A WALKING
DRESSED 1191
$25.00 PER SET

Ginny's sooo big in her smart turquoise outfit of cotton cord. Long pants and middy top with sleeves and V-insert of jersey, printed with her very own name. She carries an 8" Ginny dressed just the same.

DOLL
DRESSED 1192
$25.00 PER SET

How beautiful Ginny is dressed in a party frock of sheer white nylon with flary skirt and taffeta petticoat. Over it a tailored cropped jacket of crimson glow velveteen with pearly buttons. And isn't little 8" Ginny sweet in her companion outfit?

1500 25c Pretty little shoes and socks in assorted colors.

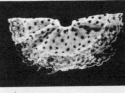

1510 50c Separate ruffled petticoats from Ginny's Petticoat Lane come in assorted fabrics and colors.

1599 $2.00 Hard-covered book of "Ginny's First Secret" 9 x 11" fully illustrated in color.

1501 25c pr. Ginny's sandals and slippers come in two styles each in assorted colors.

1509 25c Matching birthday aprons for Ginny and her little mother in white with pink designs.

1730 $5.00 Ginny's pretty Party Packages contains Ginny dressed in panties, shoes and socks plus three outfits and Ginny's Stationery.

1502 25c Ginny's handbag, beads and bracelet set in gay assorted colors.

1505 25c Five-piece fitted miniature suitcase.

1506 25c Ginny's rain bonnet and boots in transparent plastic.

1960

1610 50c Golden heart shaped locket and matching chain.

1503 25c Personalized coat hangers in colorful molded plastic. Set of 5.

1561 $1.00 New wigs for Ginny — two styles, each in three colors, Blonde, Brunette, Auburn.

1750 $10.00 Week-Ender Package contains Ginny dressed in pretty outfit and four other ensembles.

1611 50c For Ginny and her "mother" — matching pearl beads and bracelet.

1504 25c Ginny's personalized headband and matching gloves in a gay array of colors.

1560 $1.00 Five Piece Beach Roll Set has bathing suit, towel, pail and beach roll, with swim fins and face mask.

Vogue Dolls

1569 $1.00 Ginny's little play-puppy with colorful plaid blanket coat.

1512 50c To wear yourself — a Ginny, Ginnette and Jill charm bracelet.

1507 25c Plastic hooded raincape in gay rainbow colors.

1506 25c Ginny's personalized parasol that really works comes in pretty assorted colors.

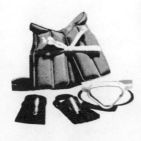

1511 50c Colorful life jacket swim fins and face mask.

3503 25c Plastic eyeglasses and case.

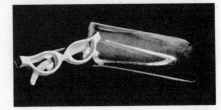

1960

FACTORY: 184 COMMERCIAL ST.
            MALDEN 48, MASS.

NEW YORK
SHOWROOM: 200 FIFTH AVE.   ROOM 656
            NEW YORK 10, N. Y.

INCORPORATED

FASHION LEADERS IN DOLL SOCIETY

 ginny

 baby dear

 ginny baby

 littlest angel

 dream baby

 ginnette

 brikette

1961

We herewith present the new 1961 line of the world-famous "GINNY DOLL FAMILY." As you study this catalog, we trust that you will note the changes and revisions that are designed to step up your sales and, more particularly, your profits with a complete line of quality dolls of proven saleability at full mark-up and full profit. The famous "GINNY" and the adorable "GINNETTE" appealing as ever to provide rapid turn-over and increased profit from minimum display space. The lovable "LITTLEST ANGEL" with proven sales where she is displayed properly as miniature dolls should. The bewitching "BRIKETTE" with that special appeal for your special customers. Darling "GINNY BABY" from 12 in. to 20 in. at popular prices. And, the incomparable doll hit of the present . . . . the all-new, life-like 18 in. "BABY DEAR" now with a 12 in. size and separate clothes to boost sales and profits.

The "GINNY DOLL FAMILY" of 1961 . . . . truly the "PROFIT LEADERS IN DOLL DEPARTMENTS" at full mark-up and full profit for all. To back up this ever-popular doll line, we continue our pledge of quality, service, and integrity and the uninterrupted rapid handling of orders to keep you in stock right through the Christmas selling season.

Your Doll Department is not complete without the profitable "GINNY DOLL FAMILY"—now packaged simply and conveniently in uniform, durable, window boxes for easy display and saleability.

Cordially,

EDWIN W. NELSON, JR.
President

1961

18430 OUTFIT $1.00
Ginny is comfy warm for bed time in her full-length cuddly pink flannelette nightie.

18431 OUTFIT $1.00
For anytime, a favorite with Ginny is a white pleaty skirt with colorful yoke.

18432 OUTFIT $1.00
Ginny loves fun time in durable play slacks and her own "Ginny" jersey sweater.

18438 OUTFIT $1.50
A "must" for every wardrobe is Ginny's comfy camel coat with brass buttons and cuddle-scarf.

18240 DRESSED $4.00
18440 OUTFIT $2.00
Ginny adores her red check French school smock, with blue lego-tards and red rollerbrim.

18241 DRESSED $4.00
18441 OUTFIT $2.00
It's party time and Ginny steals the scene in her frosty blue nylon, petticoat and straw hat.

132

the original "Fashion Leader in Doll Society" and the inspiration for the fabulous "Ginny Doll Family." I'm 8 in. tall and can sleep, sit, stand, kneel and walk. My twelve adorable outfits are sure to keep me popular with little girls everywhere.

G
i
n
n
y

18235 DRESSED $3.50
18435 OUTFIT $1.50
Look at Ginny! She's wearing her fashionable lace trimmed choir girl top and red velvety pants.

18236 DRESSED $3.50
18436 OUTFIT $1.50
Ready for school, the choice for Ginny is a willow green cotton frosted in white.

18237 DRESSED $3.50
18437 OUTFIT $1.50
For afternoon tea, isn't Ginny sweet in her cheery rosy check with organdy and lace.

UNDRESSED $2.00
18020, 18021, 18022,
18023, 18024, 18025
Two hair styles—angel cut or braids—in blonde, brunette or auburn, dressed in panties, shoes and socks.

18242 DRESSED $4.00
18442 OUTFIT $2.00
Tops with Ginny is her sunny yellow pinafore dress with perky white straw with fluffy feather.

18245 DRESSED $4.50
18445 OUTFIT $2.50
Happy Ginny in her bridal gown of tulle and taffeta with chapel length veil and bouquet.

18246 DRESSED $4.50
18446 OUTFIT $2.50
It's dress-up time in Ginny's velvety red frock and bonnet with lacy pantalettes.

18250 DRESSED $5.00
Ginny wears a Nun's habit of black broadcloth with golden cross hung from her waist.

1962

ever-popular *Ginny*

"*Fashion Leaders in Doll Society*"

Continuing to fill a need and generate sales, the world famous Ginny is a must in every prestige doll department, with a complete wardrobe of popularly priced sure-sell outfits. Her short, but sure-fire line makes her easy to display in minimum space for rapid turnover and top profits.

Courtesy of Vogue

Dressed in panties, shoes and socks, with either bangs or braids in platinum, brunette or auburn—$2.00.

For slumber-time at home or visiting, Ginny is a love in her dainty print two-piece pajammas.
Outfit only 18330 $1.00

For summer playtime or picnic fun white cotton deck pants with red print overblouse are just the thing.
Doll 18131 $3.00 Outfit 18331 $1.00

For school or play, a simple basic cotton with lace-trimmed collar is a fundamental must.
Doll 18132 $3.00 Outfit 18332 $1.00

For school, Ginny adores her sunny yellow cotton with soft green velvet sash and yellow rosebuds.
Doll 18135 $3.50 Outfit 18335 $1.50

For a change for school, a simple light blue basic with crispy white eyelet embroidered apron is perfect.
Doll 18136 $3.50 Outfit 18336 $1.50

No wardrobe is complete without a pretty pink lace trimmed felt coat with matching cuddle cap.
Outfit only 18339 $1.50

For a country fair or special wear, Ginny wears her provincial lace-trimmed red print ensemble.
Doll 18140 $4.00 Outfit 18340 $2.00

Party best for adorable Ginny is a ruffly white organdy dress with colorful flowered banding and lace.
Doll 18141 $4.00 Outfit 18341 $2.00

For cool weather play, flowered aqua jersey knit leotards and beanie with matching pixie felt top.
Doll 18142 $4.00 Outfit 18342 $2.00

Visiting best finds Ginny in her red and white candy-stripe pinafore dress with saucy straw skimmer.
Doll 18145 $4.50 Outfit 18345 $2.50

A Sunday stroll brings loving glances in a pink organdy and felt ensemble with poke bonnet.
Doll 18146 $4.50 Outfit 18346 $2.50

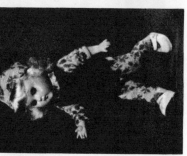
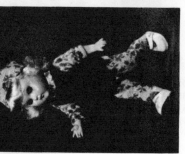

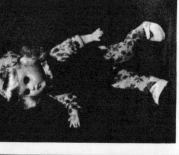

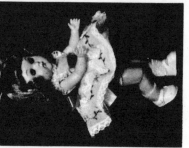

and sweet *Miss Ginny*

A companion to Ginny is our all new 16 inch Miss Ginny, the sweetest girl doll ever produced. Her two-piece plastic body and jointed limbs make her the girl doll with the most play value and appeal. Tilt her head, twist her waist, — and her wardrobe of outfits matched to Little Ginny gives her incomparable display value guaranteed to create top mark-up sales.

For school, she matches little Ginny in her sunny yellow cotton dress with soft green velvet sash and yellow rosebuds and flouncy ponytail.
Doll 86180 $8.00 Outfit 86380 $2.00

For cool weather play, she dresses like Ginny in flowered aqua jersey knit slacks and kerchief in matching pixie felt top with elfin hairdo.
Doll 86181 $8.00 Outfit 86381 $2.50

In visiting best, Miss Ginny and little Ginny are matchmates in their red and white candy-stripe pinafore dress with saucy straw skimmer.
Doll 86100 $10.00 Outfit 86300 $4.00

For the girls' club meeting, a bright rose velvety jumper dress with white nylon blouse will be the envy of all.
Doll 18137 $3.50 Outfit 18337 $1.50

Around the house on cooler days calls for Ginny's aqua cord slacks with matching angel top.
Doll 18138 $3.50 Outfit 18338 $1.50

Here comes the bride in her full nylon gown with chapel length lace veil, cap and traditional bouquet.
Doll 18150 $5.00 Outfit 18350 $3.00

For collectors, Ginny is dressed in a traditional nun's habit.

Doll only 18151 $5.00

135

Famous *Ginny*

"Fashion Leader in Doll Society" created by VOGUE

The "original" miniature doll that continues to set the standards again features a hard plastic unbreakable body with walking features and bending knee with a soft vinyl head with sleeping eyes and rooted hair. In her brand new pixie and side pony tails hair styles she'll continue to command a strong following and profitable sales.

Courtesy of Vogue

DOLLS

and sweet *Miss Ginny*

The most reliable, pliable 16 inch girl doll ever produced. Tilt her head, twist her waist, adjust her arms and legs for the sweetest, most displayable, most playable doll on the market.

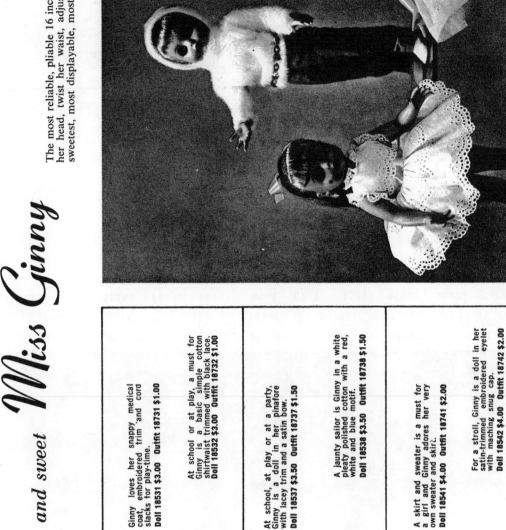

Dressed in panties, shoes and socks with platinum, brunette or blonde pixie rooted hair.
Undressed Doll 1820-1-2 $2.00

For slumber-time, home or visiting, Ginny is cute in her long plisse nightie with lace trim rope-tie.
Doll 18530 $3.00 Outfit 18730 $1.00

Ginny loves her snappy medical coat, embroidered trim and cord slacks for play-time.
Doll 18531 $3.00 Outfit 18731 $1.00

At school or at play, a must for Ginny is a basic simple cotton shirtwaist trimmed with black lace.
Doll 18532 $3.00 Outfit 18732 $1.00

For picnics or walking Ginny loves her fringed rodeo dress with bright print cuffs and fringed bandana.
Doll 18535 $3.50 Outfit 18735 $1.50

Isn't Ginny sweet in her perky lace-trimmed apron dress with the snappy checkered flair skirt.
Doll 18536 $3.50 Outfit 18736 $1.50

At school, at play or at a party, Ginny is a doll in her pinafore with lacey trim and a satin bow.
Doll 18537 $3.50 Outfit 18737 $1.50

A jaunty sailor is Ginny in a white pleaty polished cotton with a red, white and blue motif.
Doll 18538 $3.50 Outfit 18738 $1.50

Ginny is a saucy little miss for a stroll in her lace-trimmed felt coat and pillbox hat.
Outfit only 18739 $1.50

Cool snaps are fun for Ginny in her snappy flower-trimmed, hooded fleece jacket and rose cord pants.
Doll 18540 $4.00 Outfit 18740 $2.00

A skirt and sweater is a must for a girl and Ginny adores her very own sweater and skirt.
Doll 18541 $4.00 Outfit 18741 $2.00

For a stroll, Ginny is a doll in her satin-trimmed embroidered eyelet with maching snug cap.
Doll 18542 $4.00 Outfit 18742 $2.00

Dressed in panties, shoes and socks with platinum, brunette or blonde double pony tail rooted hair.
Undressed doll 1823-4-5 $2.00

For party best Ginny is beautiful in rose-trimmed velvet and nylon, matching bonnet and lace petticoat.
Doll 18545 $4.50 Outfit 18745 $2.50

Here comes the bride in her full nylon gown with chapel length veil, coronation cap, traditional bouquet.
Doll 18550 $5.00 Outfit 18750 $3.00

Ginny is dressed in a traditional nun's habit.
Doll only 18551 $5.00

With a flouncy bow on her pony tail, Miss Ginny is adorable in her white satin-trimmed embroidered eyelet.
Doll 86590 $9.00 Outfit 86790 $3.50

Cool snaps are fun for Miss Ginny in her flower-trimmed, hooded fleece jacket and hot pink cord pants.
Doll 86580 $8.00 Outfit 86780 $2.50

In party best, with long curly bob, in rose-trimmed velvet and nylon, matching bonnet and lace petticoat.
Outfit 86700 $4.00

Doll 86500 $10.00

1964

famous Ginny

famous GINNY—the "original" miniature doll with the separate wardrobe, this little 8" charmer features bending knees, walking, and rooted hair. She walks, she sits, she kneels and she sleeps. Undressed dolls $2.00; dressed dolls from $3.00 to $5.00 and clothes from $1.00 to $2.50. Ginny is a tiny toddler molded in the image of all sweet little girls.

1965   Courtesy of Vogue

Ginny	18130	18131	18132	18135	18136	18137	18140	18141	18142	18143	18145	18146	18150
White Ginnette		28130	28131		28132		28135	28136		28137		28140	28141
Negro		28030	28031		28032		28035	28036		28037		28040	28041

Ginny

Ginnette

Li'l Imp

Li'l Dear

White Li'l Imp		31140		31145		31146		31147		31150		31151		31160
Negro			31040		31045		31046		31047		31050		31051	31060
Li'l Dear		47130		47140		47141		47142		47150		47159		40125 Bunny Hug

1965 GINNY FAIRY-
TALE LAND:
Top row from the
left; Red Riding
Hood, Mistress
Mary, Mary Had
A Little Lamb,
Jack and Jill,
Cinderella and
Little Bo Peep.
FAR-AWAY LAND:
Middle row;
France, Ameri-
can Indian,
Ireland, Ty-
rolean Miss,
Scotland, Lit-
tle Dutch Girl,
Oriental, Spain
and Italy.
HISTORY LAND:
Bottom row
showing vinyl
Jill; Colonial
Days, Revolution-
ary Days, Frontier
Days, Southern
Belle, Victorian
Era and the Gib-
son Girl.

Fairytale Land			100	101	102	103	104	105		
Far-Away Lands	200	201	202	203	204	205	206	207	208
History Land			300	301	302	303	304	305		

Courtesy of Vogue

1966 *Ginny*

1966 GINNY: Top row in everyday togs and Nun, far right.
Middle row, from left; Red Riding Hood, Mistress Mary, Mary Had a Little
Lamb, Jack and Jill, Cinderella, Little Bo Peep, Wee Willie Winkie,
Twinkle, Twinkle Little Star, Hansel and Gretel. This is FAIRYTALE LAND.
Bottom row from left: Ireland, Mexico, Scotland, Little Dutch Girl and
Boy, Spain Italy, Tyrolean Girl and Boy, Scandinavia, Belgium and
Germany. Pictured to the right are France and American Indian. This
is FAR-AWAY LANDS.

139

Ginny Dolls from "Far-Away Lands"

8" Ginny and Ginnette

1820	1821	1822	1823
1824	1825	1826	1827
7820	7821	7822	7823

Vogue photos

```
      500      501      502      503      504      505
 506      507      508      509      510      511
      512      513      514      515      516      517
 518      519      520      521      522      523
```

1968 GINNYS Numbers 500-523 as follows: FRANCE, AMERICAN INDIAN, IRELAND, MEXICO SCOTLAND, LITTLE DUTCH GIRL, RUSSIA, SPAIN, ITALY, TYROLEAN GIRL, AFRICA, SCANDINAVIA, SOUTH AMERICA, GERMANY, MIDDLE EAST, POLAND, GREECE, INDIA, STEWARDESS, PILGRIM, COWGIRL, NURSE, BRIDE and NUN.

Photo right: 1968 Ballerina with original tag on wrist. This is number 8 Ginny, all vinyl, made in U. S. Costume is yellow net and chiffon with gold trim. The rooted hair is braided and worn around her head. To the best of my knowledge, this is the only Ginny that had this hair do. Below is Irish girl, 1967, also #8, in green taffeta with lace trim and lacey cap. Courtesy of Marge Meisinger.

VOGUE ♥ DOLLS'
wonderful world of miniatures

Ginny Dolls — collector series
—from Far-Away Lands

Petite 8" dolls dressed in authentic native costumes from around the world. Appealing to collectors and little girls everywhere.

> 501 — American Indian
> 502 — Ireland
> 503 — Mexico
> 504 — Scotland
> 505 — Little Dutch Girl
> 506 — Russia
> 507 — Spain
> 508 — Italy
> 509 — Tyrolean
> 511 — Scandinavia
> 513 — Germany
> 517 — India
> Dressed dolls only $7.00
>
> Factory Pack — one dozen
> Weight — 8 lbs.

Hours and hours of fun — and multiple sales — with the "original" miniature dolls and their undressable and washable wardrobes.

8" *Ginny* — the "original" miniature

Famous GINNY — the first miniature — with her fully-jointed all skin-soft vinyl body, rooted hair and sleeping eyes. Still a favorite.

#522 $7.00   **#523** $7.00

#1850 outfit	$4.00 1.50	#1851 outfit	$4.00 1.50	#1852 outfit	$4.50 2.00	#1853 outfit	$4.50 2.00
#1854 outfit	$4.50 2.00	#1855 outfit	$4.50 2.00	#1856 outfit	$5.00 2.50	#1857 outfit	$6.00 2.50

8" *Ginnette* — her baby sister

Tiny GINNETTE with her delicately sculptured hair is just the right size for little girls from 3-5 years old. All non-toxic vinyl.

#2850 outfit	$3.50 1.50	#2851 outfit	$4.00 2.00	#2852 outfit	$4.00 2.00	#2853 outfit	$4.50 2.50

Factory Pack — one dozen   Weight — 8 lbs.

Vogue photos

1970'S

In 1971 Vogue offered LITTLE MISS GINNY as COLLECTOR DOLLS FROM "FAR-AWAY LANDS" in a dozen different costumes. This was a 12" all vinyl doll with sleep eyes (some had brown eyes), rooted hair and jointed arms and legs. Old favorites such as Littlest Angel, Ginny Baby, Baby Dear-One, Baby Dear and 15" Miss Ginny continued, as well as the line of wardrobe trunks.

Joan Cornette had been the Vogue designer since Virginia Carlson had retired and she carried on in the fine tradition of Mrs. Carlson and her mother. Vogue was finding it increasingly difficult to produce Ginny and her outfits economically in the United States and began negotioations to have the doll and clothes manufactured in the Far East. All the large dolls and their garments were still being made in the United States and this continues to be true. By way of explanation, it takes just as much time and labor to produce the small doll and her clothing as it does the largest of dolls. By 1972 Ginny was manufactured in Hong Kong using the same 1966 mold for the vinyl doll that had been made in the United States. The new doll was marked GINNY on the back of the head and VOGUE DOLLS (copyright) 1972 Made in Hong Kong on the back.

Vogue Dolls became a subsidiary of Tonka Corporation in 1973 but operations were continued in Melrose MA. A GINNY PACKAGE was one of the first dolls to come out of Hong Kong; this doll had a blue velvet jumper with blouse and two separate outfits. 8" GINNY COLLECTOR DOLLS FROM "FAR-AWAY LANDS" appeared in costumes of a dozen different foreign countries. All of the dolls in the early '70's were still in production.

By 1975 fifteen Ginnys from Far-Away lands were being produced along with several new dolls: WASH-A-BYE BABY in 12" and 16" sizes and MISS GINNY CONTEMPORARY, a 15" redesigned modernday Miss Ginny, poseable and dressed in mod clothes. Several of the earlier dolls were also carried over.

In 1976 Ginny was called FRIENDS FROM FAR-AWAY-LANDS and there were twelve different countries, some of the previous year were discontinued and new ones added. Several new dolls were introduced including 12" PRECIOUS PENNY, 10" and 15" BABY WIDE EYES, both all vinyl, drink and wet characters with either rooted or sculptured hair; and 16" and 22" HUG-A-BY BABY, a cloth body doll, with sleep eyes and a crying voice. Miss Ginny came in some ravishing bridal and formal gowns that year and Littlest Angel was stylishly dressed, again by Joan Cornette.

Vogue Dolls, Inc., became a wholy owned subsidiary of Lesney Products Corporation in 1977, and operations were moved to Lesney's headquarters in Moonachie, New Jersey. Lesney continued the Friends From Far-Away Lands series and twelve were on the market including an American LITTLE PIONEER GIRL for the first time. New dolls that year included a redesigned GINNY BABY, eight inches tall with SHOWER N'BATH: a 16" BABY BURPS that drinks, wets, bubbles and actually burps; and MY VERY BEST FRIEND, a 5]/2" poseable, bendable doll with a house. The regular Vogue line of Ginny Baby, Baby Wide Eyes, Precious Penny, Hug-a-Bye, Baby Dear, Littlest Angel and Miss Ginny were carried over, too.

The LESNEY-VOGUE 1978 line included several entirely new dolls such as: PATTY CAKE SINGS, a 17" doll with rooted hair, hand painted eyes and a mechanism to clap her hands while she sings two different songs; WINKIE,, a 17" soft body doll with vinyl head and hands, rooted hair - squeeze her hand and she winks - squeeze the other hand and she blinks; WELCOME HOME BABY, a new born life-size 18" baby with a cuddly foam body and soft skin: a boxed GINNY BABY with layette; and SOFT SUE, a one piece foam body toddler, 16" tall with pony tail rooted hair and sleep eyes.

Several traditional Vogue dolls like the Drink n' Wet babies, Hug-a-Bye Baby, Baby Dear, Littlest Angel, Miss Ginny were carried over as were Friends from Far-away Lands in familiar costumes but now with painted eyes. Also, there's a new version of MISS JILL now 15" tall, attired in fashions of yesteryear.

The biggest surprise was the introduction of an entirely new concept of the 8" Ginny doll. The company announced that Ginny has been updated for the NOW look. She is a poseable, all vinyl doll with rooted hair of polyester-nylon in a brunette shade and sandy blonde in different styles and has sleep eyes. New features include: 22 changes of outfits including formal, party, sports, school, leisure and period styles; the World of Ginny Accessories with bed and bedding, wardrobe with drawers, dressing table, student desk and even a moped all designed in a durable plastic and most attractive.

This doll was unveiled at the New York TOY FAIR in February 1978. The new line was fully promoted nation-wide and generally available throughout the country. New outfits were added in 1979.

1980's

The year of 1981 saw the newly redesigned offerred as Ginny by Sassoon with a whole new line of wardrobe changes. In addition there were Ginny Far Away Lands available. In 1982 twelve new Ginny Brides along with the internationals appeared with newly designed outfits which were considered some of the nicest by collectors. Vogue also offerred 5½" Glitter Girls with different jewel colored gowns.

Unfortunately by 1982 Vogue Dolls (Lesney) was troubled financially and went into receivership. There was some hope that another company would be able to take over and still produce Ginnys but in 1983 there had been so definite announcement.

And, so this is the GINNY DOLL STORY, a full half century; from her roots in Germany, like many Americans, up to today's vinyl construction. Many dolls have come and gone but Ginny had endured through the ages to delight both little girls and collectors alike. Even in times of economic recession there is hope for improvement and that Ginny dolls will continue. MAY THERE ALWAYS BE GINNY DOLLS!

Photo by Lia Sargent

GINNY DOLLS FROM HONG KONG: Featured are Ginny dolls from Far-Away Lands. Shown
on the display board above on the top row, from left, are: MEXICO, IRELAND, TYROLLEAN,
SWITZERLAND. Bottom row: GERMANY, LITTLE DUTCH GIRL, SCOTLAND, FRANCE, SPAIN. The
three pictured on our cover are the newest in the series introduced earlier this year.
POLAND is at the top and ITALY and SCANDINAVIA are on the bottom row (from left).
All photographs are courtesy of Vogue Dolls, Inc., a subsidiary of the Tonka Corp.

The present dolls, according to Mr. Edwin W. Nelson, Jr., President of Vogue, are
modeled after the "original" Ginny. The body and legs are "blow molded" vinyl and
the arms and heads are "rotational molded" vinyl. This differs only from the
American-made 1965 doll in that the earlier one was entirely "rotational molded"
vinyl. The company has found that the "blow molding" process eliminates the pos-
sibility of one leg being longer than the other and/or having the chest concave
because of the head and wig. "The new process provides us with a better quality
product that will stand by itself and "stand up" from a quality point of view," advised
Mr. Nelson.

1974

144

GINNYS made in Hong Kong and available from 1975 to 1977. Above and clockwise: AMERICAN INDIAN, RUSSIAN GIRL, CANADIAN and AFRICAN. (Photos courtesy of Vogue Dolls, Inc.)

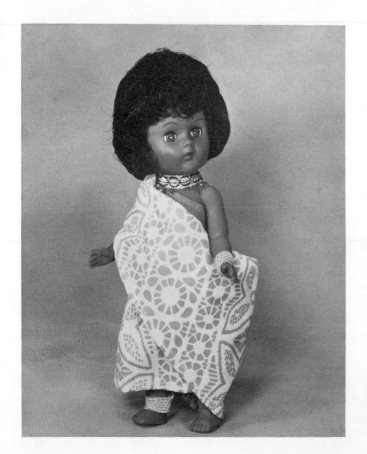

The Ginny Doll 1953

GINNY
1978

146

THE GINNY DOLL IS BACK. SHE DIDN'T GET OLDER, SHE GOT BETTER.

Ginny, the most popular doll of the 50's is back. And like the 50's themselves, she'll be an even bigger hit today.

First of all, a lot of the little girls who fell in love with her back then now have little girls of their own. And let's face it – like mother, like daughter.

And Ginny still has the same beautiful features that endeared her to so many when she was first born.

Unlike other dolls who are made-up to look like teenagers or grownups, Ginny is a little girl doll. And she's still a perfect size 8 (8 inches that is). Two more reasons Ginny is one in a million.

What's more, to make sure Ginny is comfortable in today's world, there's what we call "The World of Ginny.™"

With everything from tenniswear and ski clothes to jumpsuits and long party dresses, Ginny probably has a more varied wardrobe than your wife does. She also has a lot of other accessories. Like a bed, closet, vanity and a moped. You see, no grass grows under her feet.

Or under ours either. We'll be continuing to add to our little girl's number of clothes and furnishings.

Speaking of numbers, Ginny comes in three different price ranges. According to her outfits. Besides that, her outfits can also be purchased separately.

Ginny. She's from Vogue. She's already been established. She's got a world of clothes and accessories. And most amazing of all: she's 25 and doesn't look a day over 7.

Vogue photos

GINNY.™
FROM VOGUE® DOLLS.

The World of Ginny™

1978 Vogue photos

The wonderful World of Ginny will bring back the fun of yesterday to the mothers of today. The precious doll that mother played with as a child is now back for her little girl to play with and to treasure just as she did.

B.
B.
B.
B.

301944 Asst. "B"
Pack: 2 Dozen
8 Styles, 3 pcs. ea.

C.
C.
C.
C.
C.
C.
C.
C.

301977 Asst. "C"
Pack: 1 Dozen
6 Styles, 2 pcs. ea.

148

The World of *Ginny* Accessories

Ginny, this year, has five play accessories that every little girl will have to own.

302083
Student Desk

302096
Vanity

203097
Moped

203088
Wardrobe

302084
Bed

To create her very own bedroom there is a bed with a pretty floral blanket and pillow, a chair and dressing table will reflect Ginny's image while her beautiful hair is being combed, a wardrobe to hold all of Ginny's beautiful fashions and accessories and a desk and chair, fully equipped for Ginny's study.

Ginny also has her very own moped which comes with a helmet and basket where Ginny can carry some of her favorite accessories.

149

Ginny has been updated for the now look and comes dressed in the fashions that every little girl dreams of having today. Ginny is an 8" fully poseable doll with knees that bend so she can sit and play on any one of her accessories. She has sleeping eyes and long beautiful hair. (Note: Black doll is called Ginnette™)

301930
Ginnette

301911 Asst. "A"
Pack: 2 Dozen
4 Styles, 6 pcs. ea.

1978
Vogue
photos

150

The World of Ginny™ Fashions

301777 Asst. #2 (Carded Dresses)
Pack: 2 Dozen
6 Styles, 4 pcs. ea.

Ginny has two assortments of dresses beautifully packaged for fast sales. Each carefully designed fashion comes with its own accessories to enhance the outfits. Shoes, sneakers, ice skates, ballet shoes, hats, socks, tights and panties are all among her many accessories. Each individually styled to match her costumes.

301744 Asst. #1 (Carded Dresses), Pack: 3 Dozen, 12 Styles, 3 pcs. ea.

1978

ABOUT THE AUTHOR

Jeanne Du Chateau Niswonger is a native of Indiana, grew up and attended high school in Charleston, West Virginia, and has lived in numerous states including New York, Washington, D. C., North Carolina and Florida where she has made her home for the past 22 years. She married a physician, Dr. Joseph K. Niswonger, and there are three children. A graduate of Miami University in Ohio, she received a bachelor's degree in zoology. She also holds a master of arts in sociology and earned her Doctor of Philosophy degree in anthropology from California Western University. She also did post graduate work in social psychology at the Washington School of Psychiatry.

The author has worked as a research biologist and for over a decade was a newspaper writer for the TAMPA TRIBUNE and contributed to the NEW YORK TIMES and other publications. She has served in editorial capacities for the FLORIDA

MEDAUX, IMPERIAL MEDICAL BULLETIN, FLORIDA NATURALIST and is currently doing editorial work for a national folk dance publication and writing feature articles for DOLL READER, a national periodical for doll collectors.

Mrs. Niswonger has always been interested in civic affairs and has worked in community projects with organizations such as hospital and medical auxiliaries, county council of parents and teachers and she serves as merit badge counselor to the Boy Scouts of America. She has held office in the American Association of University Women and was on the board of directors of the Polk Public Museum.

Nature and conservation have been a special life-long love of the author. She organized the Lake Region Audubon Society, served as president for a number of years and continues on the board. The Nature Conservancy elected her as a state president in 1970 and she became involved in preserving wilderness areas throughout Florida. She has been on the board and advisory council of the Florida Audubon Society and was the recipient of that organization's Order of Eagle award. She is currently on the board of directors in the Florida Wildlife Federaation and holds memberships in the National Wildlife Federation, National Audubon Society, Friends of the Sea Otter, Defenders of Wildlife, Florida Zoological Society and many other conservation groups.

The author's biography appears in WHO'S WHO OF THE SOUTH and SOUTHWEST, WHO'S WHO OF AMERICAN WOMEN, 2,000 WOMEN OF ACHIEVEMENT, WORLD'S WHO'S WHO OF WOMEN, WHO'S WHO IN THE SUNSHINE STATE, INTERNATIONAL WHO'S WHO IN COMMUNITY SERVICE and others.

Mrs. Niswonger's hobbies include photography, reading, crafts, sewing, gardening, folk dancing, animals, music and, of course, doll collecting and researching. In 1973 she organized the Ginny Doll Club, a corresponding club for doll collectors, and serves as its president. She has held membership in the United Federation of Doll Clubs, Inc., since 1971 and was recently appointed to its Board of Governors; she also served on the steering committee of this group's 1974 national convention. She has been president of the Tampa Doll Club and recently organized a new U.F.D.C. club, the Tropical Doll Study Club, and is currently president of it. A graduate of the Lifetime Career School, she has a certificate in Doll Technology.